DEMCO

FATAL VOWS
The Tragic Wives of Sergeant Drew Peterson

Joseph Hosey

FATAL VOWS

The Tragic Wives of Sergeant Drew Peterson

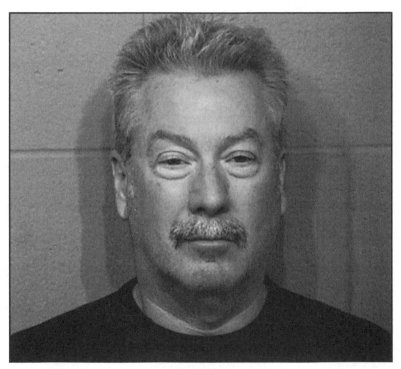

Drew Peterson—May 21, 2008 / Will County Sheriff's Department

ISBN-10: 1-59777-606-8
ISBN-13: 978-1-59777-606-6
Library of Congress Cataloging-In-Publication Data Available

Book Design by: Sonia Fiore

Cover Photography: AP Images/ M. Spencer Green

Printed in the United States of America

Phoenix Books, Inc.
9465 Wilshire Boulevard, Suite 840
Beverly Hills, CA 90212

10 9 8 7 6 5 4 3 2 1

For Gracie

"He knows how to manipulate the system, and his next step is to take my children away. Or kill me instead."

—From a letter dated November 14, 2002, from Kathleen Savio to Will County Assistant State's Attorney Elizabeth Fragale regarding her estranged husband, Sergeant Drew Peterson.

PROLOGUE

W*alter Martineck hardly knows Drew Peterson, a retired police sergeant in the Chicago suburb of Bolingbrook, but he's a good friend of Peterson's stepbrother, Tom Morphey. So it was that Martineck found himself unwittingly drawn into the events of October 28, 2007, the day Peterson's young wife, Stacy, was last seen. The prologue that follows is a dramatization based on an account Morphey reportedly gave to police, as well as statements Martineck made in the media regarding his strange run-in with Morphey late that day, before Martineck had heard a word about Stacy's disappearance. In the months that she's remained missing, numerous stories have flooded out from both those who knew her well and those who barely knew her; stories that the police, and everyone following the case in the national news, are sorting through to answer the vexing question: What happened to Stacy?*

Drew Peterson set a cup of coffee in front of his stepbrother, who was slumped in a stuffed chair in the back of Starbucks, away from the wide windows looking out onto busy Weber Road. Tom Morphey sipped the coffee and waited to hear why Peterson had summoned him there.

But Peterson only said, "Drink this. You look like you need it."

Morphey could believe he did. He'd woken up that morning with a familiar dull ache behind his eyes and burning in his stomach after spending the day on the couch, watching the Bears give away a game to the Lions. Then he dozed off and might still have been asleep if his stepbrother hadn't called at 5 o'clock that evening, asking to meet him at the Starbucks midway between their homes in the Chicago suburb of Bolingbrook.

Peterson told Morphey to be there at seven; it was important.

Morphey heaved himself off the couch and, since he had nowhere else to be, headed over to Starbucks, happy for the chance to help his stepbrother for a change. Usually it was Peterson coming through for him with things like money, furniture, or work. Just the other day Peterson had told him he could probably line up something at the local Meijer department store; Morphey needed the job, and it would not have been the first that Peterson had helped him get.

When Morphey walked into Starbucks, he was early for their meeting. Peterson was already there, sitting in back, reading the paper.

After getting Morphey coffee, Peterson asked, "How's things at home?"

Morphey just shrugged and asked about Peterson's three boys, daughter, and wife, Stacy. Peterson gushed about the kids: Tom at the top of his class and playing trumpet in the school band, Kris a champion junior high wrestler, Anthony and Lacy adorable and growing up fast. About Stacy—his fourth wife, mother to Anthony and Lacy, stepmother to Tom and Kris—he said nothing. He fell silent and stared across the table.

"Why aren't you working tonight?" Morphey asked.

"Taking the day off." More silence. Then: "I need something."

So he didn't just want to talk, to get something off his chest. He—Drew Peterson, Bolingbrook police sergeant, enforcer of law and order—needed something from his troubled, unemployed stepbrother. It was the best Morphey had felt in a long while.

"What?" he said quickly.

"Stacy," Peterson said. "She said she's leaving me again. You know how she is."

Morphey said he knew.

"It's like this every month," Peterson said. "Right around her period. It's getting to be too much. Especially since Tina."

Stacy's half sister, Tina, had died about a year before. Peterson had told Morphey how hard Stacy had taken it, about her depression, her pills. Morphey, too, knew a little something about depression and pills.

"You know what else?" Peterson said. "I think she's running around on me."

"Get out of here."

Peterson pulled out his wallet and opened it to a picture of Stacy, in a tight party dress, leaning over Drew as he sat on a chair. "You'd say no to this?"

"She's a fox," Morphey agreed, "but that doesn't mean she's running around."

Peterson put the wallet away. "It's getting to be a problem," he said. "She's a problem. We got to dispose of the problem."

Morphey didn't know what to make of that. He didn't really want to know. Had he even heard his stepbrother correctly? He didn't try too hard to figure it out.

Peterson rubbed his temples and pushed back his hair. "I need you to wait here for a little while." Then he reached into his jacket, pulled out a cell phone and handed it to Morphey.

"Take this. Whatever happens, don't answer it. Just stay here. Don't fall asleep. Get another coffee, whatever. Just don't leave and don't answer the phone. And don't call anybody either. Think you can handle that?"

"Yeah, Drew."

Peterson left. Morphey studied the phone. It was a nice one, but Morphey did not mess with it. He did not want to screw up. He sat there and tried to stay awake.

After about half an hour, a jolting ring made Morphey drop the phone in his lap. When he picked it up, he saw the caller ID.

Stacy.

Morphey stared at the phone until it stopped ringing. He didn't know what was going on, but suddenly he wasn't so sleepy.

Another half hour passed before Peterson reappeared. When Morphey asked where he had gone, Peterson told him that he just went to run an errand.

Morphey handed back the phone. "Your wife called."

Peterson put the phone in his pocket without looking at it. "I know," he said. "You did a good job."

Out in the parking lot, Peterson said, "Give me a call tomorrow. I might have something on that Meijer's thing." He got in his GMC Denali and drove off.

A few hours later, he called Morphey again. "You think you can come over here? I need a hand moving something. The Denali and the Grand Prix are in the driveway, so just park in front. You're all right to drive, right?"

Morphey put on his jacket and headed for the door. He told his girlfriend Sheryl he'd be back in a minute; he had to go to Drew's.

When he got to Peterson's house, his stepbrother opened the front door before Morphey had a chance to ring the bell. As Morphey stepped inside, Peterson glanced around the sleepy cul-de-sac. It was a few days before Halloween. The air was crisp, the house almost as dark as the street.

The kids were sleeping, and Peterson said Stacy was out with her sister. Morphey thought that was strange, since both cars were parked in the driveway. Maybe Stacy's sister had picked her up from the house.

Morphey followed Peterson upstairs and into the bedroom. He noticed a blue plastic barrel next to the bed. The barrel was tightly sealed and had two plugged holes in its lid, maybe openings for a pump. It looked a little smaller than a fifty-five-gallon drum.

Peterson squatted and put his fingers under the edge of the barrel's bottom. "I'll tip it," he said. "You take it from the top."

He pushed the barrel over, and Morphey accepted its weight. It was warm against his hands. Peterson backed out of the bedroom and toward the stairs. Morphey walked after, holding up his end. The barrel was not very heavy, and now Peterson bore all of its weight as he stepped backward down the stairs.

Morphey asked what was in the barrel.

"Chlorine," Peterson said.

Morphey thought it was strange that Peterson would have a barrel of chlorine for his swimming pool all the way upstairs, next to his bed. He wondered for what reason it needed to be moved late on a Sunday night, not to mention why it felt warmer than the air in the room. But he didn't ask any of these questions. He told himself to just believe his stepbrother, to go along with it and show himself capable of helping with this simple task.

Once downstairs, they carried the barrel through the attached garage and out to the driveway, where Peterson set it down to open the back of his Denali. The two men hoisted the barrel into the car. Peterson wedged a piece of wood against it to keep it from rolling around.

"Well, I better get this out of here," he said.

"Where you going?" Morphey asked.

"I know a guy wants to buy some chlorine," Peterson said.

"Now?"

"He wants it pretty bad." Peterson pulled a wad of bills out of his pocket and palmed it into Morphey's hand.

"Ah, Drew, come on," Morphey protested. "You don't have to."

"Got to run," Peterson said as he climbed into his Denali and closed the garage door from inside his car. Morphey watched the door go down, then drove home.

In his kitchen, he sat down and had a few drinks. His head throbbed. *Dispose. Problem.* He had a few more and then walked up the street to the home of his pal Walter Martineck. Lights shone through the front window, so he knocked on the door.

Wally opened the door, and Morphey blurted out, "I think I just helped move Stacy with Drew."

Wally tried to follow what he was saying, but Morphey was drunk and rambling, nearly incoherent. He kept trying to push a handful of money onto his pal. Wally refused and asked where the cash had come from. Morphey wouldn't say. He left his friend standing mystified in the doorway and walked back to his own house.

When he woke up the next morning, his girlfriend told him something that he already knew, no matter how much he tried to convince himself otherwise. So he went back to bed and tried to forget; he tried to pretend that it had never happened.

When he awoke the second time and couldn't fall back to sleep, Morphey swallowed a handful of pills and chased them with what was left in a big plastic bottle of liquor. The rest of that day, October 29, 2007—the day that Stacy Peterson was reported missing, as his girlfriend had informed him in the morning—was largely lost to Morphey. And as he gratefully drifted off again, he hoped the whole thing had been a bad dream.

Waking up in a hospital room in Naperville, the next town over, was no dream. Through his haze, he heard people saying he had tried to end it all with liquor and pills. He believed what these people were saying, never mind that he could not quite make out what they looked like. Whether he had intentionally tried to kill himself, which was entirely possible, or had simply overdone it trying to block out the terrible thoughts racing through his mind, Morphey didn't know or care. They gave him drugs to sleep, which was nice, but when the drugs wore off, an unwelcome consciousness returned. He slept and woke, and upon one woozy resurfacing, Drew Peterson had materialized next to his bed.

Peterson, catching Morphey's eye, leaned over and asked, "How you feeling?"

CHAPTER ONE

Inked into the flesh of Yelton Cales is the sad history of his troubled family. It's an incomplete history, still without an ending, but tattooed tributes to dead relatives already cover much of Yelton's upper body. On his left arm are the names of two of his four sisters, Jessica and Lacy. They died as young children. Scrawled indelibly on the left side of his neck is his mother's name, Christie. She is probably dead too, although no one knows for sure; she hasn't been seen or heard from since she walked away from her family, clutching her Bible, in March of 1998.

One name absent from Yelton's skin is that of his little sister Stacy Peterson, who was last seen at her home in the Chicago suburb of Bolingbrook on October 28, 2007. Maybe Yelton didn't add Stacy's name because he hoped she would be found quickly. More likely he didn't have the work done because at the time that she vanished, he was in prison for violating parole on a sex-crime conviction. When he was freed in June 2008, however, and Stacy was still missing, it looked like he might need to add another tattoo to his living book of the dead.

Yelton's body is a testament to the adversity that he and his sister, Stacy Peterson, faced from a young age, but the tattoos tell only part of the story. They don't tell about the mother who, before leaving for good when Stacy was fifteen, regularly took off for long stretches of time. They don't tell about the reportedly heavy drinking of both parents, or of how Stacy and her siblings were left to fend for themselves for weeks on end as teenagers. The tattoos don't tell the full story, even, of the man who bears them, a registered sex offender whose run-ins with the law pained his sister, although she still loved and tried to help him. And they don't tell of the loss of Stacy's adored half sister, Christina—called Tina to distinguish her from her mother, for whom she was named—who succumbed to colon cancer in September 2006, when Stacy was a young mother of two, stepmother of another two, and the fourth wife of a much older police officer.

When Stacy Cales, at the age of nineteen, married forty-nine-year-old Drew Peterson, overnight sergeant of the Bolingbrook Police Department, he must have seemed to offer the stability, respectability and authority she'd rarely known in her tumultuous early years.

It didn't turn out that way. Soon after Tina died, by many accounts, the Petersons' marriage went on the rocks, and several people say Stacy talked about taking her four kids and leaving Drew. Then, slightly more than a year after Tina's death, Stacy went missing, without the kids. All along, Drew Peterson has maintained that Stacy, repeating her mother's pattern, abandoned the family for another man.

The Illinois State Police, however, saw it differently from the beginning. Within two weeks, they had ruled Stacy's disappearance a "potential homicide," and their sole suspect was, and still is, Drew Peterson.

The same day the state police declared Stacy's disappearance a potential homicide, the Will County state's attorney also reopened an investigation into an event in Peterson's recent past that to many had always felt unsettled and mishandled: the death of his third wife, Kathleen Savio, to whom he was married when he began romancing the then-seventeen-year-old Stacy. Three and a half years before Stacy vanished, Savio, with whom Peterson was still embroiled in contentious divorce proceedings even though by then he had married his much younger girlfriend, was discovered dead in her home, in a dry bathtub. State police investigated and pretty swiftly concluded that Savio had slipped in the tub and died accidentally. A coroner's jury upheld that ruling. Peterson was never a suspect, and the whole episode was behind him in about two and a half months. But when Peterson's next wife disappeared, the death of his third spouse suddenly took on a more suspicious appearance. Her body was exhumed for another look, and this time a different conclusion was reached: Savio's death had been no accident, but a homicide.

Unless Stacy Peterson turns up somewhere, with a plausible explanation of where she's been all this time, her exit from the world will be much like her entry into it and a great deal of the time in between: marked by tragedy and family troubles.

Stacy Cales was the third child born to her mother, Christie, and father, Anthony, of Downers Grove, a suburb of Chicago, Illinois. Yelton came first, followed by Jessica, the sister Stacy never met because she died in a house fire before Stacy was born.

Stacy's aunt, Candace Aikin of El Monte, California, said the little girl was about a year and a half old when she suffered burns and smoke inhalation during a December 1983 fire in the family's ranch home. Christie Cales, who was about a month away from giving birth to Stacy, managed to escape from the burning house through a window, barefoot and in her pajamas. Her husband, Anthony, wasn't home at the time of the fire.

"My sister called me when the paramedics were taking her daughter out of the house," Aikin recalled. "She said, 'They're taking my daughter away.'"

Cruelly, the family suffered another terrible loss not long after. In October 1987, when Stacy was three and the family had added two more daughters—Cassandra, age two, and baby Lacy—Lacy fell victim to sudden infant death syndrome. After the loss of her second daughter in less than four years, Christie Marie Cales' life seemed to spiral out of control, and she became an intermittent figure in Stacy's upbringing.

After her tragedies, Christie "had a history of vanishing for weeks on end," according to the missing persons Web site the Doe Network, dedicated to investigating and solving such cold cases. She moved to the south suburbs to live with family members and saw her children only periodically.

According to a November 26, 2007, article in the *Chicago Sun-Times*, Christie Cales also suffered from depression and spent time in a psychiatric institution. While she was on the outside, Christie ran afoul of the law. One of her criminal convictions was for contributing to the neglect of a child: She had let Yelton, then seven, outside in the snow without adequate clothing.

"Cales...admitted to drinking a case of beer a day and drew convictions for many criminal charges," the Doe Network site says. "DuPage County warrants [were] issued for her on charges including criminal damage to property, battery and drunken driving."

In 1983, the *Sun-Times* article reports, Christie sought a protective order against her husband, saying he had threatened her with a .357-caliber pistol. Anthony Cales was charged with aggravated assault, but his wife refused to testify against him, so the charges were dropped. The couple seemed to have reconciled, because five months later they bought a ranch home in Downers Grove, the same one that burned down only a few months later.

In November 1989, the *Sun-Times* article also states, Christie pleaded guilty to shoplifting a bottle of vodka and three packs of cigarettes from a drugstore. The day after Christmas that same year, she was arrested for stealing two cases of Old Style, a bottle of Baileys and more cigarettes from a food store.

Eventually, her husband, Anthony, filed for divorce and custody of the children, according to the Doe Network site. In 1990, Christie at first challenged the filing but then failed to show up to court for divorce hearings, so Anthony's request for divorce was granted. "Not showing up for court was typical behavior for her," the Doe Network says.

When Stacy was fourteen, her mother picked up her Bible, said she was going to church, and left. But this time her absence wasn't just for weeks. It was apparently permanent, because she hasn't been seen or heard from since. No one knows exactly what happened to her.

"I think she went with another guy and just got in a bad situation," Candace Aikin said. "She had a habit of disappearing." Still, Aikin adamantly believed that Christie, who was forty when she vanished, is dead, not living a new life with a new identity or anything like that. True, she had taken off before, but she always surfaced eventually.

Aikin also believed that her sister, for all of her troubles, could have held it together if not for the horror of losing a second child. She recalled a visit years later to the Bolingbrook home of her niece, Stacy, during which Stacy's husband Drew took the family, including Stacy's father, out to dinner. Aikin remembered the lament of her former brother-in-law.

"He felt like if we wouldn't have lost Lacy, the second child, they would still have been together," Aikin recalled Anthony Cales telling the table. "He said, after the first death it was hard. After the second death, she lost it."

Aikin said that after Lacy died, Anthony Cales took his surviving children, Yelton, Stacy and Cassandra, down south to Florida and possibly Louisiana. For a few years she lost track of the family. They moved frequently, and she didn't always know where they were or, when she did know, why they were in a certain place.

"He didn't let us see [the children]," Aikin said. "I think he was hiding from my sister more than anyone."

But Aikin said her access to her nieces and nephew resumed when Stacy's half sister, Tina, tracked them down somewhere in the South.

"It wasn't too long, a couple years," Aikin said, relieved to find her big sister's children once again.

Although Aikin didn't live close to her nieces and nephew, she said she always tried to keep close tabs and have a positive influence on their lives, "because I was like a mother to them." Aunt Candy was the closest thing they would have to a mother, at least for a part of their lives—particularly for Stacy.

"Stacy was like a daughter," Aikin said. "I was very close to her."

Even before their mother up and left, however, Stacy and her siblings had less than ideal childhoods, growing up without much parental oversight. After her parents divorced in 1990, her father married Linda Cales, in Florida, about five years later. Stacy's former stepmother has said Anthony Cales was an abusive alcoholic, and their home was no place to grow up. The couple and the kids moved around to different places—not always, it seems, living together—shuffling around the South with periods back up in Illinois, before eventually returning to the Chicago area for good. Anthony and Linda are now divorced.

Sharon Bychowski, Stacy's next-door neighbor in Bolingbrook, who became a close friend and confidante of Stacy's in the last few years before she disappeared, recalled some of the tales Stacy told about growing up in the Cales family.

"He drinks a lot," Bychowski said of Stacy's father, while Stacy's mother "was kind of into drugs a lot." She and Drew Peterson said Anthony Cales worked in construction, but Aikin said he was a plumber. According to the Web site A Candy Rose, which has been tracking the case of Stacy's disappearance, at one time Anthony Cales had plans to buy a marina in Florida, but ended up back in Illinois.

Bychowski said Stacy had told her that their father left her, Yelton and Cassandra alone for three weeks (her parents were divorced by this time). "And they went to school every day," Bychowski said. "They got up and dressed, took showers. [Stacy] was twelve or thirteen, I think she said. She was still in grammar school.

"I said, 'You got up and went to school every day for three weeks?' I said, 'How did you have enough food?' [Stacy said], 'We ate mac and cheese, and we ate whatever we had.' I said, 'Nobody knew that you guys were alone?' She said, 'No. We didn't want to be separated.' So she's got a lot of background."

Bychowski said Stacy related that episode as the two women were returning from an outing in rural north central Illinois.

"We were going out to see my niece Jennifer—she lives in Paw Paw," Bychowski said. "They went out with me to a picnic. On the way back, me and Stacy were in the front seat, and we went by that area and she said, 'You know, I used to live here. As a matter of fact, we were here for three weeks by ourself.' [sic] And she told me that story."

Bychowski remembered pressing Stacy as to why the three children, when left to fend for themselves, did not seek help. "She said, 'But we knew that if we told somebody, we'd be separated.' I said, 'My God, Stacy, how much did you grow up?'"

After her mother disappeared and her father proved to be a less than responsible parent—having separated from Linda by this time—foster care apparently became a greater likelihood for Stacy and Cassandra. (Yelton, more than four years older than Stacy, was probably old enough by then to be on his own.) To avoid that, Stacy, by then in high school, went to live with her half sister Tina, about eight years her senior. Tina was the daughter of Christie and, according to Aikin and Bychowski, a man named Ron Kokas, whom Christie never married. At least for some of her growing up, Tina was in her mother's care; at other points, she was in foster care, according to Tina's friend Steve Cesare.

Nonetheless, by the time Stacy lived with her, Tina was married and in her twenties. Perhaps because they shared a mother who had left them behind, Tina in turn became a surrogate mother for Stacy, who lived with her sister during Tina's divorce from her first husband and after she married her second husband, Jamie Ryan. Aikin said Stacy was living with Tina and Jamie when she took up with Drew.

Stacy's sister Cassandra was also lucky enough to escape foster care. She was taken in by her employer, local businesswoman Pamela Bosco, who became Cassandra's legal guardian and, after Stacy disappeared, served as the family's spokeswoman. Years later, Bosco admitted that she regretted not taking in Stacy as well. But by that time, Cassandra's older sister was already out in the world. She had graduated from Romeoville High School in 2001—a semester early, according to her Aunt Candy—had found a job as a hotel desk clerk, and was about to meet Sergeant Drew Peterson.

Stacy, Aikin said, grew up fast. But despite the tumult and hardship she suffered from her very first days, she didn't give in to defeat or gloom.

"She was more of a softy," Aikin said of Stacy. "She still had her frustrations and everything. But she tried hard, she tried very hard, to make her life positive."

Indeed, a theme that repeatedly comes through from those who knew Stacy is that while she endured a tough childhood, she was not hardened by it. Messed up as her family was, she never turned her back on them and probably felt especially devoted to Cassandra and Yelton, after the siblings had looked out for one another for so many years. Stacy took school seriously and aspired to become a nurse, starting classes at Joliet Junior College the fall that she vanished. In photos, she often appears peaceful, serene. There was something about Stacy, even when she was just a small child, that was inherently good, her aunt said.

"She was always happy," Aikin said. "She noticed people. She was a people person. Even when she was very little."

Her friend Cesare, a Chicago-area magician, knew Stacy when she was just a girl. Cesare met eight-year-old Stacy through the then-teenage Tina, who became both his girlfriend and lovely assistant. Tina was a "box jumper, because they jump in and out of boxes," he explained. "I cut women in half, stuff like that."

Cesare remembered Stacy as a vibrant, artistic girl who was very attached to her half sister.

"Stacy and Cassandra both looked up to Tina as their mother figure," he said. "When Tina got sick, it was devastating for her."

Stacy was also in need of a father figure, Cesare said, and this is apparently what led her to Peterson.

"Stacy was a good kid," Cesare said. "In my eyes, she was just a little girl who got mixed up with the wrong guy."

If anything, Stacy's troubled childhood made her appreciate the importance of family. "Stacy was the glue in that family, and she was very responsible as a child," Aikin said.

From a young age, Stacy focused on family, on keeping her own together as best as she could and then reaching out to bring them even closer once she was married and had the means to do so, Bychowski said. For example, she often hosted family get-togethers at the roomy house on a cul-de-sac that she moved into with her husband. When it came time to choose names for her own two children, she looked no further than her immediate family: Anthony for her son, after her father, and for her daughter, Lacy, after the younger sister who died as a baby.

She also made an effort to rekindle relationships among her in-laws, Aikin said.

"She brought Drew's family back together," Aikin said. "She said Drew didn't get together with his family."

As much as Stacy managed to resist the downward pull of her family's troubles, the same wasn't true of her heavily tattooed brother, Yelton. At the time Stacy disappeared, Yelton was twenty-eight and locked away in the Western Illinois Correctional Center. He had been convicted for the aggravated criminal sexual abuse of a victim between the ages of thirteen and sixteen, and he had gone back to prison for violating his parole. It was hardly his first run-in with the law, however. He'd also spent time in prison for offenses as varied as possession of a stolen vehicle and domestic battery.

As his Aunt Candace Aikin said wistfully of her nephew, "He's a stinker."

The girl he was accused of sexually abusing was actually fifteen at the time of the offense, according to the Illinois State Police. Yelton was twenty-five. A report on the incident released by the Downers Grove Police Department said that about half past eleven on the night of January 7, 2005, Yelton "forcefully assaulted" the teen in the passenger side of a vehicle.

His victim told police that Yelton "held her hands above her head and penetrated her vaginally with his fingers and also with his penis [and] also forced her to have oral sex with him as well."

Yelton took a four-and-a-half-year hit on the sex case, and now must register as a predatory sex offender for the remainder of his natural life. Prior to that, Yelton— whose non-familial tattoos include a picture of the cartoon character Yosemite Sam and a Chinese symbol on his back, footprints across his chest, a demon and a dragon on his left arm, a tribal sign on his right forearm, the letters "H.D." on his right ankle, and the prediction "Hellbound" on his stomach—got three years for possession of a stolen motor vehicle (a black 1989 Ski-Doo snowmobile the cops caught him with in January 2004) and fifteen months for domestic battery.

According to the cops, Yelton showed up at Good Samaritan Hospital in Downers Grove in January 2002 with his girlfriend, whose identity the police have withheld. She had severe head injuries. Yelton, whose arms were scratched and shirt was soaked with blood, supposedly explained that his girlfriend fell out of the back of his van. Soon after arriving, he excused himself to go back to his van, saying he would return in "a few seconds." He drove off, leaving his girlfriend behind. When Yelton later returned to the hospital, at one point a bottle of beer fell out of his freshly changed shirt.

Cursory examination by hospital staff showed the woman's injuries were not consistent with falling out of a van, police said, but an injury to her eye was entirely consistent with being struck with a fist.

As the woman regained her composure and was able to recall what happened to her, she told officers that she and Yelton had driven to Bensenville, near Chicago's O'Hare Airport, to look for a friend. When they could not find the friend, however, Yelton's girlfriend grew frightened that he was going leave her alone in a parking lot.

When she would not leave of her own accord, "Cales drove recklessly to a parking lot...and stopped the van," according to a police report. "Mr. Cales pulled the victim out of the back of the van by her ears. Mr. Cales proceeded to punch the victim in the face. The victim felt the right side of her face go numb. The victim is unsure of the events which followed after that."

Yet Stacy, once again, didn't abandon a family member, even one who had done a pretty thorough job of screwing up his life. When he was paroled on the sex charge, she helped fix up a rental home for him to live in, although he wasn't able to enjoy it long before getting sent back to prison. Yelton was released again in June 2008.

Stacy's friend Sharon Bychowski said Stacy loved her brother. But for her own part, Sharon did not hold out much hope for Yelton's future.

"Yelton—I think he's messed up," she said. "I think he had a good time partying a lot. Drew says there's nothing that would stop him from doing what he does. He would rather just get high and party than worry about the consequences. He doesn't think consequences are important. When he gets out, he's not going to be out very long. He's going to be a career jail person. [Stacy's] focus was to get him straight."

It was precisely her devotion to family that makes Aikin utterly reject the story Drew Peterson has stuck to since Stacy disappeared: His wife was simply following in her mother's footsteps, abandoning her family without a word of explanation. He in fact seemed perturbed by her irresponsible behavior, considering everything he had done to make her happy, including buying her new breasts and a tummy tuck, and springing for hair removal, corrective Lasik eye surgery and braces. He had really extended himself, and she had the nerve to leave him and four children in the lurch. At least that's what he wanted everybody to believe, that his wife gave up on her husband and the children for the sake of an extramarital dalliance, one that possibly took her to a tropical vacation spot.

Stacy's Aunt Candy didn't buy his story for a minute.

"It's the last thing she would have wanted," she said. "When you have something happen in your childhood, you try to do the opposite. Her mother disappeared. She knew how that felt. She would never do that to her children."

In the days immediately following Stacy's disappearance, Peterson mentioned the lurid story of her mother's disappearance to me and claimed there were "indications" Christie was still alive. On this topic, Aikin once again did not share Peterson's worldview. Peterson, she claimed, badly wanted people to believe that because he also wanted people to think Stacy is still alive, that her story lines up neatly with her mother's. But Aikin firmly insisted that her sister is not alive, and Stacy's disappearance is not a reenactment of her mother's.

Stacy, for one thing, did not inherit her mother's habit of disappearing, Aikin has pointed out. Making herself scarce was something Stacy's mother did quite often, but it was a stunt Stacy had not pulled even once before she vanished at the end of October 2007.

Moreover, Aikin and others believe, Stacy would not have traded in her children to further her own romantic happiness. Bychowski agreed: "She did not walk away from her little kids. She loves her babies."

Stacy knew the particular pain of being an abandoned child; she would never willingly inflict the same injury on her own children. In fact, she had spoken with Aikin about her children's futures without their mom.

"She wanted her children to be with me if anything ever happened to her," Aikin said. "Now I don't know what's going to happen to them. All her wishes got thrown out the window."

According to Aikin, Stacy sounded like anything *but* a woman planning to run off: She told her sister, Cassandra, to worry if she had trouble even getting through on the phone.

"Stacy told Cassandra, 'If I don't answer my cell, something's wrong.'"

Stacy even predicted she would go out like this. Not dead in a tub like the wife before her, but just gone, faded away.

"She thought she would just disappear," Bychowski said. "Ironic. Sometimes they say that you know what your destiny is before it even happens."

Not that Stacy was looking in a crystal ball; Bychowski thought Peterson may have threatened her, saying that he could make her disappear. "Oh, I think so," she asserted.

Clearly, Aikin believes Peterson was involved in Stacy's disappearance. She now shudders to think that, on her visits to Illinois, she so often slept in the man's bed. She slept there with Stacy, she explained, on his side of the bed, while Drew was working the overnight shift or just out on the town, being Drew.

"I slept on that man's side of the bed," Aikin said, in a voice betraying the horror she later felt. "It's insane."

As curious and repugnant as it might seem for a seventeen-year-old girl to take up with a forty-seven-year-old man who was vying for her affections while his appropriately aged wife and young sons were sleeping not far away, it undeniably set Stacy up in a pretty good situation. She gained a beautiful home and in short order a pair of healthy, adorable children, one boy and one girl. With the package came two sons Stacy inherited from the previous Mrs. Peterson and soon adopted as her own. Bychowski described Stacy as trying to go above and beyond in proving she loved the older boys enough to be their birth mother.

Stacy had made, it seemed, a nice little life for herself. And no matter how things may have devolved between herself and her much older husband, she could take satisfaction in knowing that her children's lives were infinitely more stable than her own had been.

Stacy was smart enough to grab hold of what must have seemed a golden opportunity for a teenage girl who had fended for herself and her siblings for practically her entire life. But at some point in her four years of living that dream, it turned out to be less than she expected. Either she'd had enough and fled, or else she was taken out against her will. If that was the case, and her brother was going to keep his family's story up-to-date, he'd have to find room on his skin for the name of one more departed relative.

CHAPTER TWO

S tacy Cales was a seventeen-year-old hotel desk clerk in 2001 when she made the acquaintance of a charming police sergeant old enough to be her father. Drew Peterson in fact was a father, with two boys living at home and two grown sons. He happened to be a husband as well, for the third time. But none of this stopped him from wooing the teenage girl behind the front desk at the SpringHill Suites in Bolingbrook, a moderately priced Marriott hotel right off Interstate 55 which was largely geared toward business travelers passing through the small town.

Stacy worked the overnight shift. So did Peterson, patrolling Bolingbrook's quiet streets during their darkest hours, police work that he called "cookies and milk" after a stint as an undercover narcotics officer took him to the larger, grittier city of Joliet, a dozen or so miles south.

One might think Sergeant Peterson was stopping in on the petite teenager to ensure her safety. But the real reason, he later said, was that the cop he patrolled with had his eye on another woman working at the hotel.

"My partner liked her partner, and we got together," Peterson said.

One of Stacy's former coworkers at the SpringHill Suites said Peterson made a bad impression on her. The woman, who out of fear did not want to give her name, said she was disgusted by the notion of a middle-aged man romancing a teenage girl thirty years his junior. Yet, for an older man past his prime, Peterson must have cut a dashing figure in his uniform, and he overwhelmed his young love with pricey tokens of his affection.

An old boyfriend of Stacy's also remembered Peterson showing up at the hotel to woo the teenager. Keith Rossetto, a male nurse, dated Stacy for about two months, according to his twin brother, Scott Rossetto, also a nurse. Keith and Stacy's relationship ended when he left to join the Army two days before the terrorist attacks of September 11, 2001. Soon after, Stacy took up with Peterson, although he had been hanging around her even before Rossetto departed to serve his country.

For his part, Keith Rossetto said he did not exactly date Stacy.

"We were kind of in a getting-to-know-you phase," he told me. Still, Keith Rossetto, himself about a dozen years older than Stacy, spent time with her. He went to the hotel while she worked through the night, and when things were slow, they would go outside to smoke cigarettes and talk.

During this time, Drew Peterson also dropped in, and Keith Rossetto remembers not caring much for the cop, who kept showing up at the job of the girl he was getting to know.

"I didn't like him, I can tell you that," Rossetto told me. "It was like he was trying to impress me that he was a Bolingbrook cop, and he was on a special team or whatever."

In his younger years, Peterson had been a member of the Metropolitan Area Narcotics Squad, a multi-jurisdictional, undercover drug unit. He considers his work with this team to be the finest in his law enforcement career. An episode during his time with the unit led to him not only being fired from the Bolingbrook Police Department, which had loaned him out to the unit, but also being brought up on criminal charges. Peterson weathered that storm, as he always seemed able to do. The charges were dropped and he got his job back, but it was the end of his days as an undercover narcotics agent.

All that was far behind Peterson by the time he was sniffing around after Stacy at the SpringHill Suites, supposedly so his partner could chase some other woman working there. Peterson and Stacy's romance may have been a fortuitous by-product of their colleagues' flirting, but their liaison unleashed a storm of events beyond anything even they might have anticipated at the time.

For one thing, Peterson was still married to Kathleen Savio, although nothing as flimsy as marital vows had ever stopped him from cheating on the two wives before her. And Savio, Stacy would learn before long, was not going to set her husband, and their financial assets, free without a tenacious fight. Within a few months, police cruisers responding to Savio and Peterson's domestic battles would become a common sight on the street where all three—Savio, Peterson and Stacy—ended up living.

For another, Peterson's supervisors on the police force most certainly were not as delighted as he was with his new girlfriend.

"When the department found out I was a forty-seven-year-old sergeant, and I was engaged to a seventeen-year-old, there was a big scandal," Peterson said.

Once the department brass caught wind of their involvement, the higher-ups approached prosecutors to determine if Peterson was violating sexual-abuse statutes by romancing a girl practically a third his age. Apparently, he was not. In Illinois, seventeen is the age of sexual consent, unless the older person is in a position of authority—such as a teacher, counselor, or coach—in which case the age of consent is eighteen. The state's attorney's office decided that Peterson's status as a police officer did not constitute a position of authority over Stacy.

"The state's attorney said, 'He's not doing nothing wrong,'" Peterson recalled, visibly pleased by the memory of getting the green light to carry on with his young love, whom he clearly intended to marry as soon as he was legally free of Savio.

That Drew Peterson was able to take three ladies to the altar before Stacy is evidence enough of his charisma. And with each trip up the aisle, the age difference between himself and his wife grew wider.

With his first wife, high school sweetheart Carol Hamilton, the gap in age was a mere three years. With his second wife, Victoria Rutkiewicz, it had stretched to five: her twenty-three to his twenty-eight. Then, a thirty-eight-year-old Peterson tied the knot with twenty-eight-year-old Kathleen Savio.

To put the icing on the wedding cake, Police Sergeant Drew Peterson, forty-nine, made an honest woman out of nineteen-year-old Stacy Cales in October 2003. She had given birth to their son, Anthony, not three months before they wed.

Peterson married his first wife, Hamilton, in 1974, two years after he graduated from Willowbrook High School, which she also attended. She accompanied Peterson to his senior prom.

Peterson and Hamilton had two sons together, Eric and Stephen, but divorced in 1980. Hamilton, later Carol Brown after remarrying, did not accuse Peterson of anything sinister or violent. Asked by Diane Sawyer on *Good Morning America* if there were "any signs of controlling behavior, the things that you're hearing about now?" Carol told her, "No, there really wasn't. You know, in the beginning, we just had a normal relationship."

But that normal relationship did not last.

"Apparently we somewhat grew apart, and then one day I did discover that he was having an affair," Carol told Sawyer.

Peterson also cheated on his next wife, Rutkiewicz, whom he married in 1982. By the time Stacy disappeared, Rutkiewicz was going by the name Vicki Connolly and living in the tiny downstate Illinois town of Paxton. I met with Vicki Connolly one night while she was at the home of her daughter, Lisa Ward, also in Paxton. Vicki said she did not wish to talk about her marriage to Peterson and also told me she was afraid. I spoke to Ward as well, both in person and on the telephone, and exchanged e-mail messages with her. Ward, who lived with Peterson as his stepdaughter from the age of eight until she was seventeen, said she and her mother were not interested in discussing their time with the ex-sergeant.

But Ward did go on Fox News' *On the Record with Greta Van Susteren*. To protect her identity, Ward's last name was not given, and she was shown only in silhouette. In the interview, Lisa Ward described her stepfather as "strict, extremely strict, sometimes not a very nice person" and prone to be "extreme with the punishment sometimes."

"I was hit with a belt for many years," Ward said.

She continued, saying that despite outward appearances, she knew her mother was not happy in her marriage to Peterson and that he was "abusive to my mother. He was very controlling to her, watched every move that she had made."

And just as with his first wife, Carol, Drew lost his second wife when she got fed up with his having sex with other women.

"My mom [wanted out] because he was not being faithful to her, and he had not been faithful for many years," Ward said to Van Susteren. "And I think that she knew and finally had just had it, just wanted out."

At least one of the other women Peterson was having sex with was Kathleen Savio, who became wife number three; reportedly, she didn't know Peterson was married at the time she started seeing him.

Besides being wives of Drew Peterson, Rutkiewicz and Savio had something else in common, at least according to relatives. They both thought he could kill them and make it look accidental. As Ward told Van Susteren, "I mean, I told her she doesn't have to be afraid of him anymore, but obviously, he had hurt her, you know, so badly all those years ago that she still thinks about that. He used to tell my mother that he could kill her and make it look like an accident."

When told about the threats he supposedly made against his second wife and ex-stepdaughter, Peterson, who has had no reservations about admitting his extramarital affairs, had an explanation.

"Vicki's just mad 'cause I cheated on her," he said. He also said Ward resented him for being "a strong disciplinarian."

Besides Peterson's four brides, there was the one that got away: fiancée Kyle Piry. Peterson fit her in between his first and second marriages.

Piry claims she called it quits with Peterson; Peterson says he was the one to give her the heave-ho. Either way, Piry was twenty when the four-month engagement was called off. Keeping with his pattern of ever-widening age discrepancies, Peterson was twenty-seven.

Years later, with Peterson the subject of intense scrutiny by the police and public for both the disappearance of Stacy and the mysterious death of Savio, Piry accused Peterson of stalking her and of abusing his power as a police officer to make her life miserable for ending their relationship back when they were dating and engaged to marry.

Peterson denied this, saying Piry was just bitter over their breakup and even angrier for his spurning her attempts to rekindle the romance. He went on to explain that he dumped Piry after finding out she was seeing other men and "dancing" at bachelor parties. Piry, after denying Peterson's allegations, upped her own and claimed her ex was so cheap that he recycled their engagement ring when he proposed to Rutkiewicz.

No matter what the first three wives and the fiancée he failed to close the deal with said after things ultimately broke down, they must have seen something in Peterson at the beginning. It seems young Stacy was no different.

She may have found Peterson irresistible, blown away by the dashing figure he cut in his Bolingbrook police uniform, not to mention his authoritative mustache. Or maybe it was just the attention and the gifts he showered on her: he bought her a Pontiac Grand Prix, set her up in an apartment, and furnished her new digs. Something definitely attracted Stacy to Peterson, and it was very likely a combination of both the promise of financial security and the possibility of the stable home life she'd never had.

Whatever it was, the pull must have been powerful, because judging from the heady recklessness with which they carried out their affair, Peterson and Stacy didn't appear to have worried too much about the repercussions of getting caught. Stacy even introduced her Aunt Candy to the older, married father-figure she was dating.

"I met Drew in 2001, right after she met him," Aikin said. She found the dynamics of the relationship odd but said it was not her place to discourage her niece's budding love affair.

"It was pretty crazy," Aikin said. "But she was old enough to make her own choices. There was nothing I could do.

"She didn't have a mom. She didn't have a lot of guidance. I don't mean that in a bad way. It's just how her life was."

Perhaps even more revealing of their recklessness, in their early days Drew and Stacy would tryst in the basement of the Peterson house while his wife and boys slept upstairs. Sharon Bychowski, who became Stacy's next-door neighbor on Pheasant Chase Court and instant dear friend in April of 2004, said the young woman took her to the house where Peterson and Savio had lived—just down the street on the nearly identically named Pheasant Chase Drive.

Stacy told her, "'This is where he lived, down in the basement,'" Bychowski said. "And I said, 'So wait,'—I don't know her very well [at this point]; I just moved here—I said, 'So wait, he was bringing you here to the house?' She said, 'Yes, we would go into the basement, and I would leave in the morning before Kathleen got up.'"

Just as when he was questioned about his alleged extramarital affairs while married to wives one and two, Peterson freely admitted that he and Stacy would have sex in the basement while his unwitting third wife and boys slept upstairs.

Bychowski said she was shocked by her new friend's revelation, telling her, "'Stacy, that's terrible. I don't even know you that well and I can tell you that's terrible.' She said, 'Oh no, no, Sharon. You don't understand. Their marriage was over.'"

Stacy said that Peterson and Savio, by that time, were just staying in the same house because they hadn't yet divided up their assets and neither could afford to move.

"I said, 'Wait, let me tell you what else he told you,'" Bychowski continued, and proceeded to rattle off such lines as, "We haven't slept together in a really long time" and "I'm only here for the kids."

"She said, 'How did you know that?'"

"Stacy," Bychowski told the young woman, "because every man says that kind of shit. That's why. It's standard, comes with the package."

But by the time Bychowski shared her wisdom of the male species with her young friend, it was too late. Peterson had already snared Stacy, gotten her pregnant, and married her. Their son, Anthony, was born in July 2003, and not three months later, the new parents married in an outdoor wedding ceremony.

Savio's sister, Anna Marie Doman, said she found the notion of Peterson taking up with a girl fresh out of high school creepy.

"It's like a child molester," she said. "Stacy looked like she weighed ninety pounds—no tits, no boobs. She's not a woman."

And from the get-go, she predicted their marriage would come to no good.

"Back then I said it's not going to last, because when she hits twenty-one and sees there's a whole world out there, the shit's going to hit the fan, which is pretty much what happened." Doman might have been off by a couple years, but there are many who believe her prediction was dead-on accurate.

Savio learned of her husband's philandering through an anonymous note. The revelation turned her world upside down, but Doman said her sister was not particularly surprised. In fact, she had caught him cheating before, prior to Stacy's entry into their lives.

"He had this humungous cell phone bill, and she was like, 'What the hell?'" Doman described.

The same number was listed on the bill again and again, so Savio sought her sister's advice.

"I said, 'Ask Drew. I don't know what to tell you.' She asked, and he gave her some bullshit. She called. It was some young girl named Heather."

Savio invited Heather to her home. Face-to-face, Savio informed Heather that her boyfriend happened to be married—to her—and that he had two sons.

"That girl disappeared after that," Doman said.

Clearly, whatever disapproval he faced in his choice of new love had no effect on Drew Peterson. Between playing the expansive provider and thrilling at their clandestine moments in his basement, the middle-aged Drew Peterson was, without question, quite a happy man in 2002 and 2003.

He fondly recalled the joy he felt with Stacy and her antics to attract attention to them and leave onlookers scratching their heads. For example, Stacy would grab him in public and kiss him passionately, then earnestly ask, "Do I kiss the best of all my sisters?"

It was not the only way they turned their father-daughter age difference into a game. In the supermarket, Stacy sometimes acted like she was trying to get him to buy alcohol for her and the "friends" she had left outside, loudly badgering him to buy her wine to shock other shoppers.

"She'd say, 'Come on, all the kids are waiting in the parking lot,'" Peterson recalled, smiling at the memory. He even owned a ceramic figurine of a cop and a little girl, which he displayed on a shelf behind his desk. He pointed it out and quipped, "That was me and Stacy in 1988," when Stacy would have been four years old to his thirty-four.

While Aikin said it was not her place to criticize her legally adult niece or to tell her what to do, she did say she spoke to Stacy about her affair with the married middle-aged man.

"I did talk to her a little bit," Aikin recalled. "I can't remember what I said."

Even if Aikin had spoken to Stacy more than just a little bit, she would have been working against the clock. After all, if she had plans of talking her niece out of the ill-fated romance, there was little time to do so. Stacy and Drew were on the fast track, with the young girl pregnant by eighteen and married by nineteen.

"They got married eight days after the divorce with Kathleen," Aikin said. "It was a very private wedding."

Stacy and Drew married and settled into their home on Pheasant Chase Court, a cul-de-sac at the end of the street, a mere five hundred yards away from his old home, where Savio was still living. Peterson had actually closed on his new home in April 2002, nearly a year and a half before he and Stacy tied the knot, so they did have the opportunity to set up house before exchanging vows.

The married life must have afforded Stacy the security she had lacked throughout childhood, but it also kept her tied down with the duties of a wife and mother. Before she turned twenty-one, and less than fifteen months into her marriage, she had given birth to her second child. Plus, there were the two boys from Peterson's marriage to Savio that stayed with them during visits with their father and would, before long, become permanent members of their household.

"She was out here with the kids all the time," said Bychowski. "Those kids were so important to her."

Stacy was a natural when it came to motherhood, according to her neighbor. But it took some work to get Stacy looking, or at least dressing, the part of an adult, married woman with a slew of kids to take care of and what many have called a jealous, controlling husband. Luckily for Stacy, her next-door neighbor and best friend was there to help the young girl transform into a grown woman.

"She went, in the short time I was with her, from dressing in junior sizes to dressing elegantly and changing the way she looked," Bychowski said. "She really, I feel, in three and a half years, she went from dressing like a kid to dressing like a mom."

Bychowski knew something about appropriate professional dress. As an Avon district manager with eight hundred people working for her, she had to, and she tried to impart that wisdom to Stacy.

"We would be in Kohl's shopping somewhere and she would say to me, 'Does this look okay?' And I would say, 'I probably wouldn't buy that.'

"Like it was too short, or it was too punky, you know?" Bychowski explained. "If your objective is to dress like a mom now, then what you wear has to change."

It wasn't just her clothes that transformed. After the birth of her second child, daughter Lacy in January of 2005, Stacy embarked on a series of upgrades that included breast enlargement, Lasik eye surgery, and a tummy tuck. Peterson portrayed himself as an indulgent husband, paying for the procedures.

When Lacy was born, Stacy was nineteen days shy of her twenty-first birthday. If her life had followed a different course, she might have been just a college kid hanging out with other college kids, instead of a mother of two and stepmother of another two. She still had some growing up to do. One neighbor told of Stacy wearing a bikini when she went out to cut the grass. The same neighbor said she cautioned a friend who came to her house not to look too long at Stacy or be overly friendly, because Drew was always watching.

"He would be at the door, looking out," she said.

This was not unusual behavior for Peterson, as many who were close to Stacy said. Bychowski claimed that he would follow Stacy while he was supposed to be working and when she was doing nothing more sinister than clothes shopping for herself and her children.

"He would come there in the cruiser," she said. "He would be in the parking lot of Kohl's, [asking,] 'Hey what [are] you guys doing?'"

Bychowski initially thought Peterson's suspicions were focused more on family finances than infidelity.

"At first I thought he was checking on how much she was spending, because he always picked on her for spending," she said. "It didn't matter if she bought a toothpick. It cost too much."

She soon learned otherwise.

"[He was] constantly calling," Bychowski said, telling how Peterson was fixated on his wife's whereabouts, checking on the places she was going and who was in her company when she went there.

It was strange then, that after Stacy had vanished, Peterson seemed to suddenly have little interest in tracking down her location.

"He had such an obsession and compulsion to control her, at what point did he decide to kill her?" Bychowski pondered one winter day close to five months after Stacy was last seen alive, making no secret of her theory of what had happened to her friend. However, while the state police have ruled Stacy's disappearance to be a "potential homicide" and have named Peterson a suspect, still today, he has not been charged with anything.

"After all that money he invested in her," Bychowski wondered, "at what point did she just become expendable bullshit?"

CHAPTER THREE

Bolingbrook doesn't have much in the way of heritage or tradition. It can't; it's only been around since 1965, which makes it eleven years younger than its most famous resident, Drew Walter Peterson.

The town, which was developed as a bedroom community whose first homes were priced at ten thousand dollars, is connected to Chicago by the Stevenson Expressway. According to a "History of Bolingbrook," the first residents of the mid-1960s did not always get what they thought they were paying for.

"Lesson #1 learned the hard way through teary eyes: everything you see in the model home isn't in your finished house, necessarily," the official town history says. "In the case of Dover homes that meant no carpeting or even floor tile in some area [sic] unless you paid extra. And there certainly were no trees or lawns. And not always paved streets."

When Bolingbrook was incorporated in 1965, it was a modest burg of 5,300 people in 1,200 homes. The village has been growing ever since and in 1975 became the proud home of Old Chicago, the world's first completely enclosed amusement park and shopping center. However, Old Chicago struggled and closed six years later.

By the time Peterson was in the midst of his romance with young Stacy Cales, U.S. Census Bureau estimates put

Bolingbrook's population at about 66,000. The median home value in 2005 was more than $225,000, over twenty times the price of an abode in the town's first days.

Bolingbrook features some impressive homes, but the town—essentially a series of subdivisions—has forever been a less successful, even faceless, little sibling to neighboring Naperville. More than a hundred years older than Bolingbrook, Naperville not only has some history, it also has a bustling city center. While Bolingbrook is a series of subdivisions, Naperville is home to a quaint downtown area and charming Riverwalk, which draws visitors from across the Chicago area.

"Ranked as a top community in the United States to raise children, retire and start a home-based business, the city boasts nationally acclaimed schools, the best public library system in the country, an exceptionally low crime rate and a lower unemployment rate than the state's average," Naperville boasts on the city's Web site. "In 2005, the city was once again named as one of best places to live in the United States by *Money* magazine. Naperville ranked third of 100 finalists and was the only Illinois town to make the 2005 'Best Places To Live' list." In 2006, Naperville placed even higher, coming in at 2nd on the *Money* list.

Bolingbrook might never be Naperville—contrary to its middle-class, lily-white portrayal in the media, Bolingbrook has pockets of low-income and minority residents—but in the early part of the new millennium, it was still forging its own identity. In 2002, Bolingbrook unveiled the ostentatious Bolingbrook Golf Club, a 270-acre course with a 76,000-square-foot clubhouse. The village got another jewel in its crown when the Promenade mall opened in April 2007. An upscale, open-air shopping plaza, the Promenade was an ambitious project for Will County.

In April 2002, Drew Peterson paid about $220,000 for the house he moved into with Stacy: a two-story domicile with an attached garage and above ground pool on Pheasant Chase Court in a subdivision abutting Clow International Airport, a single-runway facility whose south end practically borders Peterson's backyard. Peterson of course wasn't new to the street, and the house he had lived in with Savio was even larger, according to his third wife's sister, Anna Marie Doman.

"There were so many rooms," Doman said.

The prices of homes in the Bolingbrook area soared soon after Peterson's 2002 purchase, then swiftly plummeted. Like many homeowners living in a volatile local market, Peterson seemed quite conscious of the swooning real estate values. He often spoke of friends losing their homes due to foreclosure in the housing bust, and he urged reporters to write about this "economy crunch" instead of Stacy.

There was a time when the asphalt circle of Pheasant Chase Court served as a playground for neighborhood children to ride bicycles and race remote-control cars. That all changed by Halloween of 2007, when a caravan of television trucks and a legion of reporters set up camp across the street from Peterson's home, asking questions about Stacy's disappearance.

"This court, before you guys showed up, was a child-friendly court," Peterson said in November to a small group of reporters standing on his front step. "You guys just killed all that."

True enough, next to no children played there throughout that winter. Then spring returned, and the media had largely departed. But even with the warm weather and the lack of trucks and reporters clogging up the street, there were still few, if any, frolicking children on the cul-de-sac—one of several marked changes to the previously unremarkable street left in the wake of the Stacy Peterson story.

The house next door to Peterson's—not the one belonging to Sharon and Bob Bychowski—went up for sale in the months after Stacy disappeared. The owner listed the two-story house, built in 2003 with vaulted ceilings and a fireplace, at $259,999. The house certainly got enough exposure after it went on the market in early 2008, but probably not the kind most home-sellers would crave. With its for-sale sign planted firmly in the yard, the house made regular appearances in television news reports about notorious next-door neighbor Drew Peterson. One had to wonder if there was a buyer out there willing to pay full price for the privilege of living next to Drew—especially in a souring real estate market.

Peterson himself admitted to me that, after spending most of his life in Illinois and three decades in Bolingbrook, he wanted to move out, go "somewhere warm," but could not, because his missing wife's name was on the title of the house.

If Peterson ever does leave the neighborhood, for whatever reason, one thing is certain: The years he lived on Pheasant Chase Drive and Court, with one wife who's now deceased and another who's gone missing, won't soon be forgotten.

Kathleen Savio, the woman sleeping upstairs while Drew Peterson and his seventeen-year-old girlfriend had sex in the basement, must have been under the impression that her family life was stable, because news that her husband was embroiled in a torrid love affair is said to have hit her like a ton of bricks. After all, she learned of his infidelity from an anonymous note.

Kathleen promptly kicked Peterson out of the house, and divorce proceedings began in early 2002. Their marriage was dissolved in the autumn of the following year, about three months after Drew and Stacy's son Anthony was born, and slightly more than a week before Drew and Stacy got married. In an unusual legal move, the divorce was bifurcated, meaning that while the marriage was legally ended, the financial side of the proceedings and the division of their property would be settled at a later date. The judge permitted this so that Peterson could marry his by-then pregnant teenage fiancée.

While Kathleen may have been shocked to learn Peterson was sleeping with someone else, she had been in that situation before, just in the opposite role. Supposedly, when she started dating Peterson, she did not know that he was still married to his second wife, Vicki, whom Peterson divorced in 1992 after nearly nine years of marriage.

Within two and a half months, Peterson married Kathleen—"Kitty" to family and friends—in a ceremony at Divine Shepherd Lutheran Church. Peterson was thirty-eight, Kathleen twenty-eight.

But the ceremony took place under a cloud. Just two weeks before the wedding, Kathleen's mother died of a stroke, at age fifty-five. "It just killed her," said Kathleen's sister, Anna Marie Doman. "What a way to start a marriage."

It wasn't the day's only setback. Kathleen's father, Henry J. Savio, who was supposed to give her away, didn't show up for the ceremony. He didn't tell anyone he wasn't coming and could not be reached. The family later learned he was angry at Kathleen for an unspecified reason, although his erratic behavior wasn't entirely surprising. Anna Marie said—and her brother, Henry Martin Savio, has concurred—that her father had almost no relationship with his children while they were growing up.

Over the course of their marriage, Kathleen gave Peterson his second set of sons, Kristopher and Thomas, born nineteen months apart. Peterson already had two boys, Stephen and Eric, from his first marriage, to high school sweetheart Carol Brown, but those children stayed with their mother after the divorce and are much older than their half brothers.

After Kathleen discovered her husband's affair with Stacy and ordered him to leave, Peterson may have been out of Savio's house but, with two children between them, he was far from out of her life. By late April 2002—in a move either ill-considered or designed to make the divorce from his hot-tempered third wife as contentious as humanly possible—Peterson and Stacy set up house right down the street from Kathleen. Peterson told me he wanted to stay close to his sons. Whatever his reasons, his proximity to his estranged wife seemed only to deepen the rancor they felt for each other, which in the months to come played out for all the neighbors to see. Compared to the split of Kathleen Savio and Drew Peterson, a run-of-the-mill divorce would look like a street fight in the face of nuclear war.

The Battle of Pheasant Chase waged for about a
year and a half after the couple went to court to sever their
marriage, during which time the Bolingbrook police, i.e.,
Peterson's fellow officers, handled seventeen domestic
incidents involving Peterson and Kathleen or Kathleen and
Stacy. In one other instance, it was Kathleen alone on the
police report. Many incidents involved visitation issues
with their sons, for whose sake the embittered couple
apparently could not manage to keep up even a semblance
of civility. The boys even had to testify in court once,
according to Peterson, after he brought battery charges
against their mother.

"They were like two monkeys in a cage, poking each
other," one party familiar with the battle said of the
divorcing couple's relationship.

On top of all the calls to police, Kathleen filed for an
order of protection against Peterson on March 11, 2002,
alleging physical abuse, harassment and interference with
her physical liberty. According to a petition Kathleen wrote
by hand, Peterson called her and said that he was coming
over to the house "to deal" with her. He wanted her dead,
Kathleen alleged in the petition, "and if has to, he will burn
the house down just to shut me up."

After she dropped the kids off at school, "he came
running after me ready to beat me up," the petition
continued. "He now [waits] for me to return home to teach
me a lesson. He has [a] gun and other weapon I believe he
will use on me. He just doesn't care if he live or die [sic], or
I live or die."

Savio went on to detail abuse and violence she said
her husband had meted out during their marriage. "Several
[times], he has restrained me, held me down, knocked me
into walls, come after me with a poker, riped [sic] my
necklace off, left marks on my body all the time, threaten to
steal my kids, and desert me."

And Peterson seemingly could not be stopped,
Kathleen wrote, as she "put [a] dead bolt on [the] door, [but]
he broke through it."

A judge granted the restraining order, forbidding Peterson to enter the Pheasant Chase Drive home, come around his estranged wife, or take their children out of her care except for his two brief weekly visits with them. Peterson was served the following day with a court summons. The order instructed the process server to deliver the paper to Peterson at Bolingbrook Village Hall, which is adjacent to the police station. It also listed his badge number, 959.

The protection order, however, didn't last long; Kathleen dropped it. Peterson said he contacted her attorney and explained that he would be unable to work as a police officer because the order prohibited him from carrying a gun. Kathleen's attorney would not discuss the matter. In any event, within a month and a half, Peterson had moved in down the street with the woman who was Kathleen's replacement.

If the violence Kathleen accused Peterson of committing during their marriage had in fact happened—attacking her with the poker, tearing off her necklace, bouncing her off of walls, restraining and marking her body—Savio never called the police at the time of the alleged events. Once Peterson and she had split, however, she showed no reluctance to bring in the cops. Of the eighteen occasions on which the police were summoned to mediate the couple's disputes, only one occurred before their divorce proceedings began; Kathleen appears to have initiated contact with the law in at least twelve of them.

Her family has repeatedly said she was frightened of Peterson. In fact, less than a year into their marriage, Savio—then Kathleen Peterson—was taken to the emergency room with a head injury she said was inflicted by her husband, and which her sister said the police responded to.

According to a Hinsdale Hospital emergency department report dated April 28, 1993, Kathleen Peterson was treated after she was "involved in an altercation [with her] husband...was hit in [the] head [with a] dining room table." Her son Thomas was not quite four months old at the time.

Kathleen suffered from nausea and dizziness, the report said. The police were notified, according to both the emergency room report and Kathleen's sister, Anna Marie.

"The police were at the house before we left [for the hospital], trying to calm Drew down," Anna Marie said. "They didn't do anything."

Another of Kathleen's sisters, Susan, told of the fear Kathleen felt during her marriage to Peterson.

"She was just terrified of him," Susan said in May 2004. "He always threatened her. He had her in the basement one time. He did many, many things to her. He wished only for her to go away."

Kathleen's nephew, Charlie Doman, the son of Anna Marie, said he got along fine with Peterson while the police sergeant was married to his aunt. Charlie, who with his sister Melissa and his mother lived less than a mile from Peterson and "Aunt Kitty," even worked in the tavern the couple owned in the town of Montgomery, about seventeen miles from Bolingbrook.

After the discovery of Peterson's teenage lover and the ensuing divorce proceedings, however, bad feelings developed between Peterson and his wife's family, Charlie told me.

The police first showed up on Pheasant Chase Drive on February 17, 2002, less than a month prior to the divorce action. They arrived to settle a "mutual argument between Drew and Kathleen," according to the report, using the first names that would characterize every synopsized report in the feud, in which the combatants and the police were so well-known to one another. "Drew left the residence. Kathleen's attorney was advised by [a department] supervisor."

The next time the police were involved in the couple's running row was in April 2002, forty-one days after Peterson's divorce filing. "Kathleen showed up at Drew's residence [on Pheasant Chase Court] and started removing items from Drew's truck," according to the Bolingbrook

Police Department. "Drew came outside and Kathleen started hitting him in the back. Drew filed a report but never followed up with State's Attorney for charges."

That was only the first time Kathleen allegedly lashed out at Peterson. Five days later, on May 3, "Drew stated that Kathleen struck him, spit at him, and pushed him in the back," according to the police record. "Drew did not want Kathleen arrested."

Apparently he changed his mind on May 26. Or pressing charges could have been Stacy's idea, as "Kathleen punched Stacy in the face because she was in the car when Drew was attempting to drop the kids off," police said. "Kathleen was arrested. Independent witnesses. Drew kept the children."

Kathleen was charged with battery; her sister Anna Marie said prosecutors wanted her to plead guilty in exchange for a sentence of one year's probation. "Her response to that was, 'Kiss my ass,'" Anna Marie told me. "They tried to push her into a confession and she refused. That's my sister. When she's right, she would not have backed down. She was a tiger."

Kathleen's defiance apparently was vindicated: she later was acquitted of the charge, according to the Will County state's attorney's office. The file, however, was expunged by court order, and no record of the case exists. Years later, Peterson told me his sons lied in court about the incident "because they didn't want their mother to go to jail." He said he understood that and forgave them.

Peterson even tried to prove this to me by calling his son Kristopher in from the kitchen to speak with us. The young man, thirteen at the time, responded to his father, "Yes, sir," and walked into Drew's home office.

"You remember when Kathleen was your mother?" Peterson asked his son. He then went on to question him about his mother and her lawyer, Harry Smith, telling him to lie. Kristopher did not seem to recall any of this.

At any rate, Savio, not surprisingly, appeared to have harbored heavy resentment for the young woman who stole her husband away. On December 20, 2002, police say she called the station to let officers know "she sent Stacy a certified letter advising that she will be arrested for trespass for future violations." Peterson had likely brought Stacy along when picking up or dropping off the boys. The police summary of this incident ends simply, "Logged for documentation."

And on September 9, 2003, police said Kathleen claimed Stacy called her "several derogatory names while Drew was dropping off the children." This matter was also referred to the state's attorney's office, but no charges were ever brought.

Kathleen in turn leveled some serious allegations against her ex-husband. Police reported that "Kathleen claimed Drew broke into the house and held her against her will" on July 5, 2002. Only she did not get around to telling them about this until nearly two weeks later, on July 18. On December 5, 2002, Savio told police, "Drew is outside pounding on the door. Kathleen states the kids are sick and she will not give them to Drew." Peterson complained to the cops that day himself, reportedly saying he was "upset he was not getting [his] kids."

And then, on June 2, 2003, the police said that "Kathleen believes someone entered the rear sliding-glass door and took her diamond wedding ring and a pair of diamond earrings out of her bedroom and a camera out of the kitchen. Drew denies any involvement." This synopsis of the report ends with the unpromising line, "No witnesses or evidence."

Most of the Drew-versus-Kathleen police reports from February 2002 to November 2003 mention the couple's sons, usually regarding visitation issues or the volatile atmosphere when the boys were picked up and dropped off. One June 2002 report had "Drew claiming that Kathleen would not turn over the kids." In January 2003, "Kathleen called stating that the kids had a late doctor's appointment and that she would not make the scheduled drop-off time to Drew," according to another report. The next month, "Drew wanted to pick up the kids. Kathleen stated they were sick and she was not turning them over." In September 2003,

"Kathleen claims Drew did not drop the kids off on time," and another time, "Kathleen [is] upset that Drew is 10 minutes late in dropping off the children."

Keeping with the pattern, there was another report of "Kathleen claiming Drew has children too long," filed in November 2003.

Things must have quieted down during December and January, as no police reports were filed in connection with the Pheasant Chase feud. But then, Anna Marie said, there was little point in calling the cops. She knows, she said, because she and her family tried.

"We were hopping around here like a bunch of rabbits," she said. "It didn't do any good."

Anna Marie said they appealed to the authorities, found nothing in the way of satisfaction and resigned themselves to being unable to find justice from the Bolingbrook Police Department.

"We knew going to Bolingbrook was like talking to the wall," she said. "Actually, worse than talking to the wall."

Anna Marie said she sought help for her sister and was ignored. According to a letter Kathleen herself sent to the Will County state's attorney's office, it seems her sister was ignored as well.

The letter, dated November 14, 2002, and sent to a Will County assistant state's attorney reads as follows (errors that occurred in the original letter have not been corrected):

Elizabeth Fragale
Assistant State's Attorney
121 N. Chicago Street
Joliet, Illinois 60432

Ms. Fragale,
On three different occasions I have tried to reach you over the phone regarding charges I filed against Drew Peterson, on the date of July 5, 2002.
Note, I did contact the Police Department, and

talked to the assistant Chief Mike Calcagno, in reference to Drew Break in that same weekend. I than filed a report in regards to my safety, from Drew by two officer that arrive at my residents 392 Pheasant Chase, Bolingbrook, Il, 60490.

When I found out Mr. Peterson was having an affair with a minor at the police department, he began to get very violent. By striking me with his hand and chasing me through the house with a police stick. At that time on record, I had to get an order of protection from him.

Their has been several times throughout my marriage with this man where I ended up at the emergency room in Bolingbrook for injuries, and I have reported this only to have the police leave my home without filing any reports.

On July 5th, Mr. Peterson got into my home with a garage door opener he programmed for himself, while I was out of town with my son's. I was unaware of his presents, and was very afraid for my live. This man pop out from our living room while I was walking down stair, with a basket of laundry. I was shocked and dropped all the cloths and stood their, asking him to get out. Drew was in uniform (Swat Uniform), with his police radio in his ear. He yelled, for me to sit down and be quiet I refused and he pushed me on the stairs. He told me to move down to the third step and not to move or speak. He was very angry that in our divorce the judge ruled he would have to pay me child support. He told me he didn't want to pay me anything. (He left my boys 8 and 9, and I With many bills, up to 2,000.00 and with an 11,000.00 income tax bill, as well as 6800.00 property tax bill for us to pay. Needless to say we are without money or any credit.) He kept me in a position for a very long length of time, while trying to convince me how horrible I am, and I just need to die. He asked me several times if I was afraid, I started to panic! He pulled out his knife, that he kept around his leg and brought it to my neck. I thought I'd never see my boys again. I just told him to end this craziness and he for some reason pulled back. I didn't tell the police because I know they can't protect me from him. I know he will be back; he's now attempting to try to make me look like *the bad guy, with untrue charges of Battery against him, and his 17 yr. Girlfriend. The sick thing is I really think they're enjoying this. Over the summer they went out of their way to roller blade right in front of my home, drive by and stop for long lengths of time in front of the house. Childish things like his girl friend flipping me off if I was out in front with the kids while driving by.*

At the present time my children have been in a program at school called rainbows, in efforts to repair some of the damage Drew and his girlfriend has created. One of which Drew falsely arrested me in front of my children with my face in the grass and calling me a criminal for hitting his girlfriend, which didn't happen. Instead she called me a bounce of inappropriate name in front of my children, so I felt it was necessary to get them back in the house away from this. When I ran to the truck, it being very high up I notices Stacy his girl friend taping me, with the stolen camera Drew took from our home. I attempted to take the camera and my next goal was to return to my home with my children. But I was thrown to the ground and treated like an outlaw, and booked and arrested for no reason. My wrist was sprained, when I was being thrown to the ground and held down by Drew, who was not on duty at the time. While this was happening my children were being held against their own will, by [the following is partially blacked out, but appears to read "Stacy Cales"], while she told them to sit down and be quiet. My son's phyc is working with them but states, 'she can't fix what continue to happen on a on going basis'. My eight year old come home from spending 1 hour with his dad, because he really is never there, and pushes his sons and girlfriend on my son all the time, and expressed to me that he was confused! It seemed that Drews live in girl friend showed both my sons her wedding dress and ring, and told them she was going to marry their father. Of course that's okay, for Adults, but when my boys come home with tears in their eyes, still hoping for mom and dad to get back together again, it become heart breaking and very confusing to them. They don't understand how dad can get married if he's still married to their mommy. The list goes on, and I understand it's just part of it, but it need to stop. My sons and I would like to move away from this area, for our safety and sanctity. I am a full time Nursing Student and Drew left me while in the middle of the program. I don't want my career or my sons to suffer this nightmare anymore.

He knows how to manipulate the system, and his next step is to take my children away. Or Kill me instead.

I really would like to know why this man wasn't charged with this unlawful entry, and attempt on my life. I am willing to take any test you want me to take to prove my innocents of charges against me, and also any lie detector test, on the my statement I filed against him. I really feel, Drew is a loose cannon, he out on the streets of Bolingbrook patrolling, and just taking the law into his own hands. I haven't received help from the Police here in Bolingbrook, and asking for your help now. Before it's to late. I really hope by filing this charge it might stop him from trying to hurt us.

Sincerely, Kathleen Peterson

Kathleen had been the woman spurned, dropped by her husband for a girl twenty years younger, which certainly makes the hostility she felt toward her husband at least somewhat understandable. But the anger may also have been so intense because, as her sister Anna Marie told me, improbable as it may sound, "I think she was still in love with Drew at the end."

Yet Anna Marie mentioned another man her sister loved even more than Peterson; a man who may have been, in fact, the love of her life. This man, whom she identified only as "Mark"—she couldn't remember his last name— reappeared at a memorial service for Kathleen.

Mark was Kathleen's last serious boyfriend before she took up with Peterson, Anna Marie said. They dated for quite a while, but it just never turned into marriage.

At the memorial service, "he was just crying like a baby," Anna Marie said. "He said, 'I still love her. I should have married her. She'd still be alive.'"

Mark had never married, Anna Marie said, although he told her he "came close a couple times." As close as he came, she said he never got over her sister.

"He was really broken up," Anna Marie said. What's more, his love would not have been unrequited, had her sister been alive.

"I think Kitty was still in love with him," she said, telling how one time, when Kathleen was married to Drew and after their son Thomas was born, she'd spotted her old boyfriend on a boat on Lake Geneva in Wisconsin.

"She said, 'My heart sank,'" Anna Marie recalled.

But Kathleen's heart proved resilient, because she moved on with her life, entering into a serious relationship after her marriage fell apart. According to an Illinois state police special agent, Kathleen and her boyfriend, Steve Maniaci, even contemplated marriage. Reportedly, he and Kathleen had a phone conversation at the end of February 2004 in which they discussed wedding plans.

Maniaci failed to respond to numerous requests to speak of his past with Kathleen, his knowledge of Peterson and his fourth wife, and the phone conversation with Kathleen. If they indeed discussed their marriage plans during that phone call, it was, as it turned out, the last time they talked about the matter.

Anna Marie, however, explained that her sister and Maniaci had known each other for close to half of their lives, meeting when they were both working for a company that provided jukeboxes and pinball machines.

"She was in her twenties," Anna Marie said. "There was a bunch of them that got together. They called themselves the stinky dogs. They were all young, stupid, hanging out."

The stinky dogs might have been young and stupid, but as they aged, they obtained professional and financial success, Anna Marie said. They also kept in touch and managed to meet periodically and even went on vacations together. When she was married to Peterson, Kathleen still saw the other stinky dogs about twice a year, although her husband disapproved.

"Oh, no, he didn't like that at all," Anna Marie said. "They would bring their significant others. Drew never went."

Anna Marie said she sometimes went in her sister's husband's place. While she was out with them, she noticed the heat between her sister and Maniaci.

"There was an attraction between Kitty and Steve," she said. "It just never went anywhere."

After she split with Peterson, Kathleen and Maniaci had the opportunity to get a romance off the ground, and their future looked promising.

"My sister was very happy," Anna Marie said. "Steve's mild-mannered. He just loved the kids. I was so happy she was happy.

"She loved those kids to death," she continued. "I don't think she would have been with anyone who didn't love the kids."

Kathleen and Maniaci were together in early 2004. By then, the war between Savio and Peterson seemed to be winding down.

Then suddenly, during the last weekend of February, came an abrupt, total ceasefire.

That weekend, Peterson had his sons. He tried to return the boys to Savio at the appointed time, he said, only she was not home, or at least not answering the door.

It was unlike Kathleen to be gone when her sons were scheduled to return.

The reason for her strange absence would soon become known: a revelation that was a tragedy for her young sons and family but also spelled the sudden end of Peterson's ongoing battles—financial, emotional, civil, and criminal—with the woman up the street.

CHAPTER FOUR

Drew Peterson spent the last weekend of February 2004 with his two sons, Kristopher and Thomas; the highlight of the weekend was a visit to the Shedd Aquarium in Chicago. The boys lived with their mother, Kathleen Savio, but their dad was just down the street with his new young bride.

In a few weeks, Peterson had a court date in which he was to surrender a substantial amount of assets and property to his ex-wife. Peterson may have been remarried, and Savio may have been involved with a new boyfriend, but their divorce was not yet final. The second half of the proceedings, the part where the couple's property and assets were divided, was at last coming to a close, and it looked like Savio was going to walk away with at least the house on Pheasant Chase Drive and very likely much more.

"Drew was already skinned alive in the preliminary," said Anna Marie Doman. "She was going to get the majority." Already Peterson was paying a few thousand a month in child support, Doman said, and her sister told her she was due to get part of his pension, as well. "She was going to do pretty well," Doman said. "She wouldn't have to work after that. But she never got it. Quite a miracle."

On that last Sunday in February, his weekend with his sons over, Peterson took the boys back up the street to their mother's home. No one answered the door. It was unlike Savio to miss a scheduled pickup or drop-off; in fact, in the past she had often called the cops if he was at all late in bringing back the boys. Her unusual absence concerned him, Peterson later said. The boys stayed with him and Stacy that night.

On Monday night, March 1, Peterson again attempted to find out was going on inside the home of his ex-wife. He was on duty, in uniform, when he drove up in his squad car to his old house at 392 Pheasant Chase Drive. He rang the bell repeatedly; again no one answered. He then went next door to summon help from neighbors. A locksmith was also called, and he was able to gain entry to the home.

Peterson was reluctant to go inside. After all the blowups he'd had with his ex-wife, the fights and allegations and calls to police, he did not want to be accused of doing anything untoward. So he sent the neighbors in first. Steve Carcerano, a neighbor whom Peterson said witnessed acts of violence between him and Savio, ventured into the house along with another neighbor, Savio's friend Mary Pontarelli. They made it to the bathroom and Carcerano saw what he said looked like an "exercise ball" sitting in the dry bathtub. But it was no ball. It was Kathleen Savio, doubled over, naked and dead.

Peterson rushed up the stairs, Carcerano said, saw the scene in the bathroom and called out, "Oh, my God!" What, he fretted, would he possibly tell Kristopher and Thomas?

Peterson's colleagues from the Bolingbrook Police Department were the first to respond to the scene. It was, to say the least, an uncomfortable situation. The deceased's ex-husband was a sergeant on the force, and the couple's tumultuous history was well-documented with the department. Supervisors decided it was prudent to immediately hand the investigation off to an outside agency. That agency was the Illinois State Police.

State police detectives arrived at Savio's home and called in technicians to process the crime scene. Savio's body was then removed from the bathroom and taken to the county morgue in nearby Crest Hill.

The officers then talked to Savio's neighbors, according to Illinois State Police Special Agent Herbert Hardy, who later testified at a coroner's inquest to determine how Savio died. They spoke to Drew Peterson, and they also interviewed Steve Maniaci, Savio's boyfriend at the time. Maniaci and Peterson's ex-wife had reportedly spoken on the phone around 1 o'clock Sunday morning. She asked him to come over, according to Hardy, but he begged off, saying he was tired.

Hardy said another state agent also interviewed the ex-husband's new wife, Stacy Peterson. Years later, after Stacy had been missing for weeks and suspected by the state police to be dead at the hands of her husband, a law enforcement source said the fourth wife played a key role in keeping Peterson above suspicion in the death of number three.

"She was his alibi," the source said, but went no further.

State police didn't interview Thomas, who was eleven at the time, or Kristopher, who was nine, "just not to put them through that," according to Hardy.

At the time she died, Savio was both working and studying nursing at Joliet Junior College; she had a boyfriend with whom she was discussing marriage. She had two sons. And in a month or so, the conclusion of her divorce would bring her into a respectable haul of money and property.

So Kathleen Savio had quite a bit to live for. She did not fit the profile of a suicidal subject, and healthy women around the age of forty don't often accidentally drown while bathing.

But it was not impossible—at least the state police thought so—and that was the story they stuck to.

On May 7, 2004, six members of a coroner's jury settled into their chairs at a government building in downtown Joliet to hear testimony relating to Savio's death.

While a coroner's inquest involves witnesses, testimony and a jury, the proceeding is nothing like a court trial. The purpose is solely to determine the manner and cause of death, and jurors have only five options available to them: natural, accidental, suicide, homicide and undetermined. An inquest can be called for any death that is not obviously natural.

The jury's decision also carries no legal weight. At Savio's inquest, Will County Coroner Patrick K. O'Neil prefaced the proceedings by reminding those gathered there, "This is neither a civil nor a criminal hearing." As a statement from the Adams County, Illinois coroner's office explains, "The verdict and inquest proceedings are merely fact finding in nature and statistical in purpose."

Fewer inquests are being held these days, following a change in Illinois law that gave coroners the option after January 1, 2007, to determine the cause of death without an inquest. But in 2004, a suspicious death such as Savio's necessitated one, and a little more than two months after the discovery of her body in a bathtub, the first probe into her tragic demise was under way.

O'Neil ran the show at Savio's inquest, but the star player at the proceeding was Special Agent Hardy of the Illinois State Police. Hardy was dispatched to testify, even though he only played a small role in the investigation of the woman's death. He did not talk to Peterson or Stacy, and he never met with friends or family of Peterson and Savio. He also did not attend Savio's autopsy and never made an appearance in the second-story bathroom of 392 Pheasant Chase Drive to inspect the death scene. Yet for some reason he was the representative the state police selected to attend the inquest of a police sergeant's former wife, who died mysteriously in the midst of an acrimonious divorce, weeks away from taking her ex-husband for a good piece of his financial pie, and who had at one time filed an order of protection in which she alleged he had threatened to kill her.

Hardy did question some of Savio's neighbors but, by his own admission, not any who might provide any useful information.

"I didn't talk to the ones that were really close to her," Hardy testified at the inquest. "Myself and [another agent] did what we call a 'neighborhood canvas,' and we did speak to quite a few of the neighbors in the general area of the residence."

It came as little surprise that Hardy did not get much information out of those neighbors.

"Did anyone hear or see anything unusual, see any squad cars or anything, any suspicious activity in that area?" O'Neil, the coroner, asked Hardy.

Hardy said they had not.

"Did you find any signs of foul play during the course of your investigation?" O'Neil asked at the inquest.

"No, sir," Hardy said. "We did not."

So the tangential neighbors were not the only ones who saw nothing amiss; neither did the state police who arrived soon after the grisly discovery. There were no indications of a burglary or home invasion, no weapons in the house and, according to Hardy, no signs on Savio's body or in the home that a struggle had taken place.

"Everything seemed to be in order," he said. The only possible exception was an unmade bed with some books and magazines lying on it. "Nobody related to us that they saw anything unusual in the neighborhood those last few days."

The only unusual thing, then, was the dead woman in the dry bathtub.

"There was no water [in] the tub when our agents arrived," Hardy said. "It must have drained out after setting for such a long period of time."

Savio's hair was still wet, the special agent noted, her fingertips were pruned, and her skin was wrinkled. She had a cut on the back of her head, and a small amount of blood was in the tub.

"We think that the laceration from her—that she sustained to the back of her head—was caused by a fall in the tub," Hardy said. "There was nothing to lead us to believe that anything else occurred. There was no other evidence at this time that shows that anything else occurred."

However, Hardy never laid out a specific scenario about what state police believe immediately preceded the fall in the tub. Had Savio, at the end of her bath, stood up to unplug the drain but slipped before she could do so? Had she slipped getting *into* the tub? State police didn't say; perhaps it was not something that could be determined. The tub stopper was down—that was confirmed at the inquest—but there was no mention of having tested the stopper to see how fast a tubful of water could seep away. Would a plugged-up tub drain and dry out in less than two days, the amount of time between Savio's phone call with her boyfriend and the discovery of her body? Would a body lying in a tub trap some water underneath it that wouldn't evaporate in that time? If any of these questions factored into the state police's deliberations, the public never knew of it.

Savio, state police concluded, had fallen and drowned in the tub while water slowly drained away; she died from an accidental drowning.

"And at the point we're at now," Hardy said, "we're still waiting.... All alibis, all stories were checked as to where people were, and if I remember…if I recall correctly, the only thing we're waiting for now is some phone records to find out if certain calls were made when they said they were made. So at this point, that's where we're at." And it's at that point that they pretty much stayed for the next three and half years.

In stark contrast to Hardy's confidence in how Savio perished, her family testified at the inquest that they never for a moment believed her death was an accident. Rather, they told the jury that Savio lived in terror of Peterson.

Savio's sister, Susan Savio, said Kathleen even predicted that if she died, "it may look like an accident, but it wasn't."

"And it's just very hard for me to accept that," Susan continued, "what had happened. His reactions to this were a laughing matter—cleaning everything out, ready to get rid of the house. It's very hard."

Peterson did not attend the inquest.

Family members also brought up financial issues between Kathleen Savio and Peterson. In the divorce settlement, Savio was to get the house. Once she had it, Susan Savio said, "She was going to sell the house and move away." But Peterson had other plans, according to Savio family members.

"He said he wanted to sell her house, pay his off, and open a bar," said Anna Marie Doman, speaking up from the audience. "That's what he said at the wake, anyway."

At the inquest Doman also told of assets Peterson stood to gain if his ex-wife happened not to be alive by the time they settled the financial issues of their divorce. Peterson, she said, had taken out a hundred-thousand-dollar life insurance policy.

"She also had a one-million-dollar policy that I'm not sure if he knew that she had changed," Doman said. "He was the original beneficiary. She did change it to—down the road—to put her boys, plus the equity in her house, which was worth a little over three hundred thousand [the net proceeds were actually $287,154]. It was paid for. But he was trying to claim the whole house on joint tenancy, which should have been hers. It was pretty much a deal that was cut between them. Yeah, so there was a lot of financial gain."

While on the stand, Hardy said he knew nothing of any large insurance policies from which Peterson might have been able to profit. He didn't mention any probe of Peterson's financial gain from his ex-wife's death. But Anna Marie Doman asserted that financial gain was at the forefront of Peterson's mind.

"He wants the whole house, wanted to be named the executor of the assets, which means he would have controlled the one-million-dollar policy, and plus he also took out a separate policy himself on her, the one hundred thousand," she said.

As it happened, Peterson did not become the executor of his ex-wife's will. Instead, his uncle, James B. Carroll, was named the executor of the two-page handwritten will that coincidentally popped up only about two weeks after Savio died. It was produced by Peterson himself.

The will, which was written on lined paper and dated March 2, 1997, had Peterson and Savio leaving everything to each other, except "in the unlikely event we should die on or about the same time," in which case their two sons, and Savio's stepsons, would get to split it all up. As Peterson was still very much alive when Savio was found drowned in an empty tub, he stood to get everything.

And Carroll did right by his nephew, allegedly awarding him nearly complete control of Savio's assets even though the two were divorced, at least halfway, and Peterson was married to another woman with whom he had a child.

Of the will, Peterson said, "We just tucked it away, and I found it after she died," according to a *Chicago Sun-Times* article dated January 25, 2008. "There's nothing sinister and out of line about it. Everything was done proper." Interestingly, Savio's divorce attorney, Harry Smith, said Savio had told him that she didn't have a will. And the court-appointed administrator for Savio's estate made a statement claiming that "the actions of the Executor were not in the best interest of the Estate or its beneficiaries," calling the will itself "purported." Nonetheless, in 2005, a Will County judge accepted the will as valid, because two of Drew Peterson's friends testified that they had witnessed both Peterson and Savio sign the document.

After Stacy Peterson disappeared, three and a half years later, the state police would take a close look at the financial dealings of Drew Peterson and Kathleen Savio, but at the 2004 inquest, the topic did not appear to interest them much.

The inquest had other business to cover, anyway. O'Neil briefed jurors on Savio's autopsy, which had been performed by forensic pathologist Bryan Mitchell.

Savio's remains were delivered to Mitchell in a body bag. Save for a yellow metal necklace, she was naked, and her hands were bagged. In his physician's report to O'Neil, Mitchell wrote, "The decedent appears to be of normal development, an adequately nourished and hydrated adult, and white female weighing 154 pounds and measuring 65 in. in length.

"The hair is long, brown, and straight," he wrote. "The hair is soaked with blood. The eyes are closed.... There is a foam cone emanating from the nostrils.... The lips are purple.... The tongue is partially clenched between the teeth. Each earlobe is pierced once.... The fingernails are short and clean. There is wrinkling of the fingers and palmar surface of the left hand."

Mitchell cut into Savio's body, making a Y-shaped incision on her torso. His autopsy revealed that she had suffered from no tumors, significant trauma, infection or congenital anomalies. There was moderate pulmonary edema, or buildup of fluid in Savio's lungs, and water in the ethmoid sinuses. In his report, Mitchell ascribed the immediate cause of Savio's death to drowning. In the space on the report to list "other significant conditions contributing to death but not related to the terminal conditions," Mitchell wrote nothing.

Toxicological testing showed Savio had been living clean, free of alcohol and drugs, both street and prescription, when she died.

Mitchell did find a one-inch blunt laceration to Savio's scalp, a red abrasion to her left buttocks, three bruises on her lower abdomen, a bruise on the back of her thigh, purple bruises on both shins, two abrasions to the right wrist, an abrasion to her right index finger and a red abrasion on her left elbow. Other than the head wound, O'Neil told the jury that the injuries had been on her body for some time.

"There are six—or there are seven other bruises noted to the decedent, all of which are old. There are no new bruises noted to the decedent," O'Neil testified. He also said, strengthening Hardy's assertion, "The laceration could have been related to a fall."

The jury took it all in—Hardy's testimony, the family's version of events, and the contents of Mitchell's autopsy report. They retired, deliberated and returned to announce that they found Kathleen Savio's death to be, indeed, an accidental drowning.

The verdict stunned Savio's family. "We were all standing in the hallway like, 'Holy shit. Is that it?'" said Anna Marie Doman.

Furious that her family had been denied justice, Doman told me that after the inquest she tried to get the state police to take another look at her sister's death, but her pleas went unanswered.

"I was screaming my head off," she said. "I was calling everyone I could. I had a suitcase full of stuff. They [the state police] said, 'The coroner said it's closed. It's an accident.' I asked [the coroner's staff] more than once, 'Is there further testing you can do?' I'm thinking exotic drugs. Is there strange poison?'"

But the answer from the state police was clear: the jury's decision essentially ended their interest in the matter. As State Police Master Sergeant Thad Lillis said at the time, the jury's conclusion would likely close the investigation of Kathleen Savio's death.

And so it was for three and a half years, until Stacy Peterson vanished. Only then, after Stacy had disappeared, did anyone pay attention to the sordid tales of Kathleen Savio's marriage to Peterson and the appeals of Savio's sisters that her death had been no accident.

The same day the state police declared that Stacy Peterson's death was a "potential homicide" and named her husband Drew Peterson as their only suspect, the Will County prosecutor announced he had secured a court order to exhume Savio's body from Gate of Heaven Cemetery in Hillside, Illinois, for additional postmortem testing.

On November 9, 2007, State's Attorney James Glasgow's petition to disinter Savio's body from the suburban Chicago cemetery was granted. In his petition, Glasgow said Savio's death scene appeared "consistent with the 'staging' of an accident to conceal a homicide."

Four days later heavy equipment ripped open Savio's resting place and her leaky—or, as one police source put it, "cheap"—casket was pulled from the ground.

Savio's body was taken back to Will County for another autopsy, this one performed by forensic pathologist Larry Blum. Months passed before Blum's findings were returned to the county and his determination released to the public. During that time, another forensic pathologist, not from Will County and more accustomed to the bright lights and big stage, did an autopsy of his own. The autopsy, performed with the approval of Savio's family, was paid for with private funds, but the disclosure of the findings was quite public.

By November 16, just three days after Savio's body was taken out of the ground, Dr. Michael Baden—former chief medical examiner of New York City, author, and frequent guest on television-news shows—had reached his conclusion about how Savio died. When, after several commercial-break teasers, he announced his verdict at the end of Greta Van Susteren's program on the Fox News network that night, Susteren treated the event as though it were the Oscars and Baden held an envelope with one of the winner's names inside.

"It's my opinion, to a reasonable degree of medical certainty, it's a homicide, and that's what I would put down on the death certificate," Baden proclaimed.

While Baden's pronouncement carried no legal weight, it certainly packed a dramatic punch, given the circumstances leading to Savio's exhumation. And Baden was not done talking. Detectives and doctors, Baden said, should have realized there was something rotten afoot in 2004.

"Even initially, there was enough information that it was a homicide because of the fact that she was an adult, healthy, hadn't been drinking or anything, found dead in a bathtub. It does not happen accidentally," he said. "No history of seizures or illness. And in addition, there were indications then of multiple blunt-force traumas, of being beaten up. And one of the things we were able to look at today is those bruises [that] were still there, and we could see with the naked eye that they were fresh."

Baden's assertions of fresh bruises and an obvious homicide were a direct contradiction of the inquest testimony of both Special Agent Hardy and Coroner O'Neil. O'Neil, an elected official who is not a forensic pathologist, could say he was merely repeating what was related to him by Bryan Mitchell, the doctor who performed the initial autopsy. The state police, on the other hand, had some explaining to do.

Digging up Savio's body not only put fresh pressure on the state police—and, certainly, on Peterson—but unleashed a flurry of activity from Savio's family to right what they saw as long-ignored wrongs.

Anna Marie Doman and her brother, Henry Martin Savio, started to put a wrongful-death civil lawsuit in motion, going so far as to hire New York City attorney John Quinlan Kelly, who's no stranger to high-profile cases. He represented the parents of Natalee Holloway, the young woman from Alabama who vanished during a high school graduation trip to Aruba in May of 2005. Like Baden, Kelly frequently appeared on Fox News programs and, in fact, one night in February, 2007, was a guest on Greta Van Susteren's show that featured both the Natalee Holloway and Savio cases.

Kelly also represented the estate of Nicole Brown Simpson in a multi-million-dollar civil suit against disgraced football legend O.J. Simpson.

Like Nicole Brown Simpson's family before her, Doman suggested her family might pursue the wrongful-death suit against Peterson if the case broke that way.

"If it flies from there, that's the direction we'll go," Doman said.

Doman and Henry Martin Savio also felt emboldened enough to try to wrest control of Savio's estate from the suddenly embattled Peterson.

In February 2008, the brother and sister filed court papers to have Carroll removed as executor and replaced by themselves. They alleged that allowing Peterson's uncle to be the executor was a conflict of interest, and leveled accusations that he "wasted and mismanaged the estate."

That opinion was echoed by Richard J. Kavanaugh, who was a court-appointed administrator for Savio's estate. In January 2008, the *Chicago Sun-Times* reported, Kavanaugh said he was concerned about the way the handwritten will "just popped up" after Savio died. "It gives you the sense that it's something that's concocted."

According to the *Sun-Times*, Kavanaugh had become involved in the case because no Savio family member showed up to represent the estate in court at the time that the will was being handled, a point Peterson, in the same article, made hay of: "If they didn't like it, well, they should have done something. They didn't."

Now, apparently, there were plenty of Savio family members who wanted to be put in charge of the dead woman's estate, not only Doman and her brother but Savio's thrice-married father, Henry J. Savio, and his twenty-three-year-old son, who filed suit to be executors themselves.

Doman and Henry Martin Savio, however, asserted that they should be executors rather than their father, Henry J. Savio, whom they claimed was "unfit to serve due to hostility in that he has had no relationship with any of the children while they were growing up…failed to support them during their minority and first met his grandchildren at the funeral of Kathleen and has no relationship with them."

According to the petition to reopen Kathleen Savio's estate, Henry Martin Savio and Anna Marie Doman have, in addition to full sister Susan Savio, three half siblings from their father's two subsequent marriages, and another half sibling from their mother's remarriage. Despite the existence of Savio's full sister and four half siblings, Henry Martin Savio and Anna Marie Doman maintained that "they had the closest relationship with [Kathleen Savio] prior to her death and have been instrumental to pursuing the investigation into her death." Doman did live the closest to her sister, first in Bolingbrook—at one time living on the same street that Peterson's stepbrother, Tom Morphey, would move onto—and then in nearby Romeoville with her two children, Charlie and Melissa Doman, and Melissa's children. Anna Marie Doman also said she was vocal in her futile attempts to get police and prosecutors to take a hard, serious look at her sister's death.

She and her brother, she insisted, were not angling to strike it rich by seizing control of their sister's estate. In fact, she said, they would probably lose money when legal fees were factored in. They were doing it, she said, to ensure Kathleen's two sons, Kristopher and Thomas Peterson, got what they deserved of their deceased mother's worldly possessions.

"We'll be suing on behalf of the boys," Doman said. "People think we're making money on this. We're not."

A Will County judge sided with the Savios, removing Carroll from his role as executor in April and replacing him with Anna Marie and her father. It was but one step on the path to the wrongful-death lawsuit Anna Marie said she wanted to pursue.

Different considerations would be in play with such a civil action suit against Peterson. It might not only wound him financially but could also get him on the witness stand, under oath, so an attorney could ask him some less than comfortable questions about the circumstances of Kathleen Savio's "accidental" demise. If he was placed on the stand, Peterson said he would invoke his Fifth Amendment rights and mutter nothing that might incriminate him.

The Savio family's quest for what they saw as justice for their sister got an enormous boost on February 21, 2008, when State's Attorney Glasgow's office finally announced the results of Blum's follow-up investigation and dropped this bombshell: Kathleen Savio's death was, in fact, a homicide, not an accident.

"[C]ompelling evidence exists to support the conclusions that the cause of death of Kathleen S. Savio was drowning and further, that the manner of death was homicide," the press release quotes Blum as saying.

Blum's investigation included a review of photos from the scene of Savio's death, reports of the initial scene investigation, and an examination of the physical location of Kathleen Savio's death that he conducted on November

20, 2007. His report also included the results of microscopic examinations and toxicological tests conducted on postmortem tissue specimens, which were collected during the first autopsy, on March 2, 2004, the second autopsy performed by Dr. Blum on November 13, 2007, and Baden's autopsy three days later. Those results, however, remain part of the ongoing investigation into Kathleen's death and have not been released.

Blum's findings certainly were a gratifying development for Kathleen's family. The news even knocked the wind out of Peterson, who sputtered, "You're kidding me" and "Unbelievable" when told of the report. A day later he even admitted to being "scared." Then his bravado returned, and he and his attorney, Joel Brodsky, dismissed the new findings as having little merit, coming nearly four long years after the original autopsy found no signs of foul play.

For the time being, even with Blum's new findings, the official police record of that weekend—that Drew Peterson was watching the dolphins at Shedd Aquarium with his children when Kathleen Savio died—hadn't been disproved. But Peterson's alibi was Stacy, and she wasn't around to confirm it anymore. The state police also have not said what she told them that night.

But Stacy reportedly had done some talking about the night Drew's wife before her had died. After Stacy vanished, at least two men came forward to say she had had conversations with them about Kathleen's death. The conversations must have born little resemblance to what Stacy told the state police, because based on what the men recounted of those talks, they sounded like the farthest thing from an alibi.

Still, police and prosecutors face the challenge of tying Peterson to the crime. The new autopsy conclusions, while potentially damaging to Peterson, are far from a lock on prosecutors getting an indictment or conviction. In fact, as crime-fighting history in Will County has shown time and again, a lock of that kind can prove somewhat elusive.

CHAPTER FIVE

Five miles south of Bolingbrook on Route 53, tucked back from the road behind neatly manicured lawns, lies the sprawling Stateville Correctional Center. For decades, this has been where the worst of the worst were often sent: murderers, rapists, sex offenders. Richard Speck, who one night in 1966 systematically stabbed and strangled seven student nurses in Chicago, then raped the eighth before killing her too, was a longtime resident of Stateville until his death in 1991. John Wayne Gacy, the notorious "clown killer" who entertained neighborhood children as Pogo the Clown and ended up killing thirty-three boys and young men, most of whom he buried in the crawl space under his house, was executed at Stateville in 1994.

One of Illinois' maximum security prisons and more recently the site of a receiving and classification center which male convicts from northern Illinois pass through before being assigned a regular prison home, Stateville presents an imposing image. Spreading over 2,264 acres, bordered by a thirty-three-foot concrete wall with ten towers, and inhabited by the ghosts of thousands of hardened felons, Stateville is a potent reminder that crime doesn't pay. Yet in Will County, despite being home to Stateville, crime—serious crime—doesn't always get punished either.

Friday, November 9, just twelve days after Stacy Peterson vanished, Illinois State Police Captain Carl Dobrich announced at a press conference that Drew Peterson was a suspect in his wife's disappearance. The same day, Will County State's Attorney James Glasgow said that he was ordering the body of Peterson's third wife, Kathleen Savio, to be dug up and reexamined, to see if the state police, who had handled the investigation into her death and found no signs of foul play, missed something the first time around.

It was not a good day for Drew Peterson. In fact, it was not a good week. Two days earlier, Peterson had been called to testify before a grand jury. Still, after twenty-nine years in Will County law enforcement, he had to know that he was a long way from being dragged off in handcuffs and charged with murder. He had to know how very unlikely it would be for him to stand trial for the killing of a woman whose body no one has yet been able to find.

How can it be, many may reasonably wonder, that a man can lose fully fifty percent of his wives under mysterious circumstances and, so far, avoid arrest? In Will County, actually, such situations are not unheard of. The disappearance of Stacy Peterson was another installment of a sad story, familiar enough to have spawned a sardonic joke in the area: If you want to get rid of your wife, Will County seems to be the place to do it. It might be funny if there weren't a plentiful history of unsolved cases and criminal-justice misfires to support that view.

In November of 2007, Peterson wasn't the only guy walking around Will County with a missing wife and the cops on his back. Fewer than ten miles away, over in Plainfield, lived Craig Stebic, husband of thirty-seven-year-old Lisa Stebic, a food-service worker at an elementary school, who went missing about six months before Stacy Peterson. Lisa had mailed her attorney a letter telling him she wanted her husband out of the house so she and their two children could "live in peace." Unfortunately, the letter did not get to the lawyer until a couple of days after Lisa was last seen alive.

Stebic told police his wife walked away from their home on April 30, 2007, carrying her purse and a cell phone. A neighbor filed a missing person's report. While police have named Craig Stebic a "person of interest" in his wife's disappearance—they've searched his computer records, interviewed him, and seized twenty-four guns from his home, along with a pickup truck and a car—he has not been charged in the case. No one else has, either.

The cases of Stacy Peterson and Lisa Stebic share some striking similarities. Peterson said Stacy threatened to divorce him; Stebic and his wife were in the midst of a divorce. Lisa Stebic, according to friends, said she was afraid of her husband and was receiving counseling from an agency that provides services to battered women (claims her husband denies); Stacy Peterson had also told friends and family that she feared her husband would harm her. Family and friends of both women insist they would never abandon their children. Both husbands are suspects in their wives' disappearances, although police have not backed up their limited accusations with any action as bold as arresting either man.

Stebic has even spoken up to say he felt Peterson's pain.

"I know what he's going through," Stebic said. "Especially with you media and everything."

With Peterson, the police are contending with one of their own: a sergeant with nearly three decades of law enforcement knowledge that could help him outwit those who would put him behind bars. Stebic happens to be a pipe fitter and remains just as free, proving that you don't have to be a professional to confound the cops.

Florence Wilms has been following the news of Stacy Peterson's disappearance with particular interest. She's seen these details before: the missing wife, the husband who claims she ran off with another man, even allegations of an unaccounted-for barrel. To Wilms, who lives in the Chicago suburb of Downers Grove, the case all too eerily resembles another with which she's intimately familiar.

Wilms' daughter, Joan Bernal, disappeared in December of 1988. Days earlier, she and her husband,

Gilbert Bernal, had set out on a trip to his hometown of Edinburg, Texas. According to police, Gilbert Bernal said his wife missed her three children and wanted to return home. So he gave her $1,500, and she hopped on a Joliet-bound bus out of McAllister, Oklahoma. If she ever made it back home, no one saw her around town.

Like Stacy Peterson, Joan Bernal's body has not been found and her husband has become a suspect in her disappearance. Witnesses have claimed to have seen Joan Bernal in Chicago Heights and Tennessee; in much the same way, Peterson's lawyer claimed to have anonymous letters indicating Stacy's been sighted in the company of a man in a Peoria, Illinois supermarket and in a Kentucky shopping mall.

One of Bernal's in-laws reportedly testified that Bernal assured his wife that he could kill her, place her in a barrel, and hide her forever. Other witnesses reportedly said Gilbert Bernal bought a pair of barrels prior to the alleged murder. After his wife disappeared, only one barrel was still in his garage. When Florence Wilms heard about a barrel possibly figuring into Stacy Peterson's disappearance—Tom Morphey's as-yet unproven story that he helped Drew Peterson move a barrel the night Stacy vanished—she was astonished.

"I swear that Drew Peterson has taken a lesson from" her daughter's case, Florence Wilms told *The Herald News* of Joliet. "It sounds so similar."

Unlike Drew Peterson, however, Gilbert Bernal was arrested, even though there was no evidence of a dead body. On the strength of his in-law's testimony, and other witness statements, Bernal was charged with the murder of his wife and ordered to stand trial.

An arrest and a trial date, however, don't guarantee a trip to Stateville. After waiting eleven months to stand trial, Gilbert Bernal's day in court never came; a murder case without a body can apparently only go so far. Prosecutors set Bernal free before he was tried.

And despite intense searches that now look like an uncanny prelude to the Stacy Peterson case, no one ever found Joan Bernal, or the elusive second barrel.

Another stubbornly cold missing-wife case in Will County is the disappearance of Jeri Lynn Duvall.

Jeri was last seen alive by her husband, Bob Duvall, on June 8, 1990, when she was thirty-nine years old. The Duvalls' stormy marriage was marked by constant domestic strife, according to one of their daughters, Heather. She told *The Herald News* in a September 2, 2007 article that she remembers her father choking her mother and chasing her around the neighborhood with a knife. Heather also said that he would disable his wife's car whenever he got mad at her.

Heather was twelve and her sister, Lisa, was eight when they left to spend a weekend in Michigan with their maternal grandparents. Heather told *The Herald News* that her parents had fought before their departure, and she "didn't want to leave her with him." Her mother reassured Heather that everything was fine, but after the weekend with their grandparents, when Bob Duvall showed up to collect his children, he was sporting fresh scratches on his face and arms. Once he and the girls were at their home in Shorewood, a small town west of Joliet, he told them their mother had walked out.

It was not for another four days, after Jeri's mother insisted, that Duvall reported his wife missing to police. The police, in turn, found nothing substantive to help them locate the missing woman.

Heather moved in with her grandparents when she was sixteen, joined the military after high school, and never spoke to her father again. Lisa stayed with her father, bouncing back and forth between Michigan and Florida. She landed in a Florida prison for auto theft in April 2007. Her release was scheduled for June 2008.

Since his wife disappeared, Duvall has been arrested on charges of felony assault in Ludington, Michigan, and on charges of possession of a firearm by a felon in Shorewood. In Volusia County, Florida, he has been arrested on charges of disorderly intoxication, driving under the influence, and sale and delivery of marijuana. In contrast to the ease with which Duvall has repeatedly made his presence known to police, Jeri Lynn Duvall's whereabouts remain a mystery to this day.

Not that finding a body in Will County is any guarantee of an investigation going somewhere. Such was the case with Inge Strama, a Plainfield mother of two who disappeared in July 1993.

The Plainfield police never publicly named her husband, Frank Strama, a suspect in the case. But Strama understood that he was not above their suspicions.

"Statistically, it is the husband that's involved a lot of the time," he told *The Herald News* a year after his wife vanished. "I was a suspect, and I was interrogated several times."

Still, the police never named Strama as a suspect— even after his wife's extensively decomposed body turned up four years later in an overgrown, empty lot in the Chicago suburb of Worth, about two blocks from where her car had been spotted only hours after her husband first reported her missing. All that was left to identify Inge were her teeth and wedding band. Because of the condition of her body, investigators could not determine how she met her end.

Like Drew Peterson, Frank Strama claimed his wife ran off with another man. If this were the case, then somewhere in her running around she ended up a time-ravaged corpse in Worth. And if Inge Strama's or Stacy Peterson's "other" men ever existed, it's likely their disappearances would have resulted in missing-persons reports to match up with Inge's and Stacy's. The two men must have kept extremely low profiles before running off with their married women, however, because it seems neither man, if he does in fact exist, has been reported missing.

The Strama case was a victory of sorts, as a body was eventually found. Just getting to that point can be a tricky thing in and around Will County, even when the body has not been hidden. Take, for example, the disappearance of David Bucholz, a nineteen-year-old manager of a Dairy Queen in the city of Lockport.

Bucholz took a dinner break from the Dairy Queen one evening in July 2001 and never returned. No one saw anything of him until the next April, when his skull was found in a field near Romeoville, the next town over.

The police had been able to find Bucholz's Honda two weeks after he vanished. The keys were hanging from the ignition and a cup containing antifreeze was inside the car. Investigators theorized that Bucholz drank the toxic antifreeze and walked off to die. His body was not concealed yet still took nine months to find.

In adjacent Grundy County, eighty-five-year-old Clarence Henry was gone even longer. He likely was inside his car in the Illinois River for nine days shy of a year—despite air, ground, and river searches—before two young fishermen found a sneaker containing human remains, then noticed something in the water when a barge came through and disturbed the surface.

That something turned out to be Henry's car and what was left of Henry (who was missing his shoe and the foot that was inside of it). It was not determined whether Henry drove into the river accidentally or intentionally; regardless, it seems unlikely that he and his car were put there to be forever hidden away.

During his tenure protecting and serving, Drew Peterson worked on a high-profile missing-persons case that his department tackled, that of thirteen-year-old Rachel Mellon, who vanished January 31, 1996. The case remains unsolved. Peterson confirmed that he helped with the case but won't discuss it further.

That day in 1996, Rachel had a sore throat and stayed home from school with her stepfather, Vince Mellon. Her mother, Amy Mellon, went off to work and never saw her daughter again. During the stepdaddy and daughter's day together, the girl somehow vanished without Mellon realizing it. In fact, the first time anyone noticed that Rachel was no longer in the house was after her mother came home from work and the family was settling in for dinner.

For the first two days, Bolingbrook police considered the matter a missing-persons or teenage-runaway case—

Rachel had run away from home once before, for twelve hours—despite evidence that Rachel took nothing into the freezing January weather but a pair of slippers, the sleep clothes on her back, and possibly a blue blanket. Police then came and looked around the house, Amy Mellon said, but nothing happened after that.

Right around the fourth anniversary of Rachel's disappearance, perhaps to make up for lost time, Bolingbrook police brought Vince Mellon into the station and held him for nine hours. Officers also served a search warrant for his blood, saliva, and body hair as part of a first-degree-murder investigation.

Four days after this, Vince Mellon was trotted before a grand jury. Police also revealed that they had discovered "new information" through "technical advances," amounting to "significant developments" in the case. It looked like the investigation had finally taken off.

That was in February 2000. Whatever the new information, significant developments and technical advances may have been, they remain as great a mystery today as what happened to Rachel. Her stepfather, in the intervening years, has run afoul of the law on a variety of charges. Her mother was also picked up for theft, which involved the couple stiffing a Joliet motel out of a night's stay. Both Amy and Vince Mellon, who now live in Cleveland, Tennessee, pleaded guilty to the theft charge.

By the time Stacy Peterson disappeared, Rachel Mellon would have been a young woman of twenty-five. No one has ever been arrested or charged in connection with her disappearance. Prior to the tenth anniversary of the young girl's disappearance, State's Attorney Glasgow, whose administration handled the Mellon matter throughout its history—except for a four-year stretch following his electoral defeat in November 2000—said that Rachel's was "obviously at the top of our list as far as the cold cases we have."

Rachel's father, Jeff Skemp of the Chicago suburb Forest Park, said he's accepted that his daughter is probably not coming back, although he's never totally given up hope that she might be living somewhere no one can find her.

Skemp, who works as a cab dispatcher, remembers meeting Drew Peterson.

"I kind of liked him," Skemp said. "He was real brazen and kind of cocky. I think the whole world knows he's cocky now."

His lukewarm admiration of Peterson, however, doesn't extend to police in general.

"I just think that Will County's just inept," Skemp said. "I know Bolingbrook is. They did the same thing with Rachel that they did with Stacy. They waited a week before they went in the house." In fact, state police searched the Peterson home three days after Stacy was reported missing. Still, Skemp says, "They wait too long before they realize the seriousness of the case. They just got a terrible track record."

That track record includes not only the unsolved cases of Stacy Peterson, Lisa Stebic, Joan Bernal, Jeri Lynn Duvall, Inge Strama, and Rachel Mellon but also two high-profile Will County homicides in which police did arrest someone—only, in each case, it turned out to be the wrong man.

On May 18, 1998, state police were called into Frankfort for the first murder in the village's 128-year history. The Frankfort police asked for the state agency's assistance because they thought they were ill-equipped to lead the investigation of such a serious crime. As it turned out, the state police—the same agency now handling the Peterson and Savio investigations—didn't prove themselves any more adept.

Juliet Chinn was a forty-three-year-old, long-time employee of Oak Forest Hospital. She worked as a pharmacist on the second shift, along with her boyfriend of nine years, fellow pharmacist Barry McCarthy.

One Monday afternoon Chinn failed to show up at work, which was strange for her. She did not call in to explain her absence, which was stranger. At the suggestion of a coworker, McCarthy left the hospital and drove to Chinn's Frankfort condominium to check on her.

When he got there he found his girlfriend sprawled in a pool of blood, a rug covering her and a knife sticking out of her chest. McCarthy called the Frankfort police. When they arrived and saw Chinn's slain body, the man standing in the parking lot—McCarthy—began to look to them very much like the killer.

That night McCarthy was taken to the Frankfort police station, where officers confiscated his shoes. He was then ferried to the local state police headquarters, where he was interrogated into the morning and through the next night. Hardly recovered from the shock of finding his nine-year companion stabbed and covered in blood, he was questioned for more than twenty-four hours. Grueling and exhaustive as the interrogation was, police apparently didn't uncover enough information to hold him for another night. He was released without being arrested.

Two months later, McCarthy was back at the local state police headquarters. This time, he was arrested and charged with the murder of Juliet Chinn. To be sure, McCarthy was a reasonable suspect. He and Chinn were romantically and professionally linked, and McCarthy was at the crime scene when police arrived. Not only that, but he had blood on his hands and pants, blood that would prove key to collaring him for the crime.

According to Glasgow, private forensics expert Dexter Bartlett opined that, based on the pattern of blood spattered on McCarthy, Chinn had aspirated that blood onto him, proving she was still alive when he was with her in the condo. Glasgow had his doubts and called in Tom Bevel, a former Oklahoma City police investigator and associate professor of forensic science, to review Bartlett's findings.

Bevel did disagree with Bartlett. The spatter, he said, could have resulted from a part of Chinn's body, perhaps her hand, falling in a puddle of blood and splashing

McCarthy when he moved her to see if she was still alive. Effectively, Bevel was saying the state police had jailed an innocent man.

More than a year after McCarthy was arrested, the charges against him were dropped during a routine hearing. But despite Bevel's testimony and the dismissed charges, McCarthy knew that many people still thought he had murdered Chinn. The word of the police, he discovered, carries a lot of weight.

"You work with people for twenty years and the police come in and say, 'You killed someone,' and they believe them," McCarthy said, "because there's so much faith in the police, and it's undeserved.

"People don't know how to do their jobs," he said. "That's the problem."

Glasgow said state police investigators were upset with him for clearing McCarthy. The Frankfort police chief at the time, Darrell Sanders, who drove McCarthy back to his car after his twenty-four-hour interrogation by state police, said, "As far as I'm concerned, the case was closed, and the proper person was arrested."

About seven years passed after McCarthy's exoneration, and the police remained hesitant to accept McCarthy's acquittal. Then came further, even more convincing evidence that he was innocent: Someone else confessed to killing Chinn.

That person was fifty-two-year-old Anthony Brescia, who was in prison for the murder of a man in Palos Park, about thirteen miles north of Frankfort, four months after Chinn's murder. According to a press release put out by Glasgow's office, Brescia told Illinois Department of Corrections workers that he had killed Chinn as well. Even though the Palos Park murder took place soon after Chinn's in a nearby town during another daytime robbery, before his confession Anthony Brescia had never been considered in connection with Chinn's slaying.

In fact, Brescia's confession was something of a fluke. His mother died shortly before he came clean, according to Glasgow. Brescia had the blood of one victim on his hands, but he did not want his mom knowing he had killed another person, Glasgow said.

Brescia had another motive for owning up to Chinn's killing that was a bit less selfless, according to two well-placed sources. He wanted a television set in his cell, and he expected to get it in exchange for his testimony. One of the two sources said Glasgow didn't come through on the deal.

Whatever Brescia's reasons for confessing, corrections workers alerted Frankfort police to Brescia's statements, and in December 2005 two detectives visited him in prison and took a videotaped confession, according to the press release from Glasgow's office.

Brescia had been committing a string of daytime robberies, and on that May day in 1998, Chinn's condo was the next target. Brescia apparently didn't plan, however, for Chinn to be home when he broke in. He fled. Chinn chased him out the front door and shouted his license plate number as he started down the street. So Brescia returned, stabbed her in the neck and chest with a kitchen knife, and strangled and choked her.

He was indicted in June 2006 and, in March 2007, pleaded guilty. Anthony Brescia is now serving a life sentence for Chinn's murder.

McCarthy was vindicated by Brescia's confession, but the damage to his reputation, psyche and wallet had been done. Friends had abandoned him. He no longer worked at the hospital. He dropped more than a hundred thousand dollars in legal fees and lost untold years off his life. He was reluctant to apply for a new job for fear a background check would turn up his murder arrest. He worried about clearing customs to enter a foreign country for vacation. Worst of all, Juliet was irrevocably gone. "She's not back," McCarthy said. "So I don't need the time, to be honest with you."

McCarthy puts some of the blame for his wrongful arrest on fate, likening it to going to the emergency room when an incompetent doctor happens to be on shift. The fact that the detectives who showed up at Chinn's home that evening in 1998 zeroed in on him instead of picking up the right trail was nothing more than the "luck of the draw, basically," McCarthy said, sounding almost philosophical about his close brush with possible lifelong imprisonment or date with a lethal injection.

"It depends on who the cops are who get your case that night," he said. "If you get a couple bad ones, you're screwed."

A confession played an important role in McCarthy's exoneration. Years later, a different confession figured prominently in another widely publicized murder case in Will County—this time with disastrous results. The confession came from a father, Kevin Fox, horrifically admitting to killing his three-year-old daughter. Within hours, though, Fox denounced his confession, saying he had given it under extreme duress after fourteen hours of grilling by Will County sheriff's detectives.

The morning of June 6, 2004, three-year-old Riley Fox was discovered missing from the family's home in the little Kankakee River town of Wilmington, about a half hour south of Joliet. That morning, Riley's brother Tyler came into his father's bedroom and said Riley was gone. Kevin Fox had been alone with his children that night while his wife, Melissa Fox, was taking part in a breast-cancer walk in Chicago and spending the night with friends. Earlier in the evening, Fox had left the kids at their grandparents' while he went to a concert with his brother-in-law. When word of Riley's disappearance got out, the small town launched a massive volunteer and police search. Within hours, a pair of hikers found the little girl's body floating face down in a creek about four miles from her house. She was half naked and her mouth had been covered with duct tape. The ensuing autopsy revealed more grisly details: Riley had been sexually abused and was still alive when she went into the water.

For months, Melissa and Kevin Fox and their family cooperated with detectives. They submitted to rounds of questions and provided the police with samples of their

DNA, trusting officers in their efforts to find Riley's killer. Unknown to them, however, Kevin had become their prime suspect.

In October 2004, detectives brought Melissa and Kevin Fox into the sheriff's department and interrogated Fox for fourteen hours, without a lawyer, keeping his wife in a separate room for some of that time. By the end of the marathon session, Fox, to the shock of his family and friends, confessed to killing Riley. He made a videotaped statement in which he reportedly described accidentally hitting his daughter in the head with a bathroom door. Thinking he had killed her, he supposedly masked the mishap as a kidnapping, sexual assault and murder, and topped it off by dumping his daughter in the creek.

Fox was arrested. The very next day, Jeff Tomczak, the Will County state's attorney, announced he would pursue the death penalty. At the time, Tomczak was a week away from an election showdown with his bitter political rival, Glasgow. Tomczak's critics accused him of timing the interrogation to score a high-profile, tough-on-crime victory days before a hotly contested election (which Tomczak subsequently lost). Tomczak, Will County Sheriff Paul Kaupas, and others insisted politics had nothing to do with it; Tomczak denied knowing that the detectives were going to bring Fox in that night, much less that Fox would tell them on videotape that he violated and killed his daughter. Almost immediately after his arrest, Fox recanted his confession, which he said he gave only in desperation, after a grueling interrogation and promises from detectives that if he admitted his guilt, he could plead to a lesser charge, get out on bond and go home to his family. (The detectives denied offering any lenient treatment in exchange for a confession.) But as he learned later that day, he in fact could not bond out—he would spend the next eight months in jail. And far from any lesser charge, Tomczak was going after him for first-degree murder, which carried a possible death sentence.

Kevin and Melissa Fox consequently filed a civil-rights lawsuit that named the county, the detectives who interrogated him, Tomczak, and others involved with the case.

A key factor in their lawsuit was the delay in testing DNA evidence that had been recovered from Riley's body. Months after the crime, the evidence languished untested. Fox's attorney, Kathleen Zellner, finally secured a court order to send the evidence to a private lab for testing. The results brought glorious news for Fox and his supporters: The DNA did not match Fox's. Glasgow, who was now the state's attorney after defeating Tomczak, freed Fox. As with freeing McCarthy, it was a move that enraged many in the law enforcement community, who to this day are convinced Kevin Fox murdered his daughter. They were also frustrated that the judge in the civil suit didn't allow Fox's videotaped confession to be admitted as evidence and shown to jurors.

Then in December 2007—during the height of the media furor surrounding the Stacy Peterson investigation— the jury's decision was in: an award to Kevin and Melissa Fox of $15.5 million, an amount believed to be the highest judgment in Illinois history for a police-misconduct case. The couple was seeking $44 million.

However, the Foxes have not seen any money yet and probably won't anytime soon; the appeals process will ensure that the matter remains in court for years.

Throughout the Fox case, outside observers wondered: How could anyone, especially a father, confess to such horrible things if he hadn't done them? Steven Drizin, legal director of Northwestern University's Center on Wrongful Convictions, told *Chicago* magazine in a July 2006 article that he found nothing mystifying about a confession like Fox's. "You're overcome by grief," he said. "You're put into a cramped room and subjected to an unusually long interrogation. You're told there is overwhelming evidence against you, including a failed polygraph [Fox had taken a lie-detector test and been told he'd failed]. You're offered a less-serious offense and the chance to go home to your family and clear things up later in court. They simply broke him down psychologically to a point where he believed that the only way he was going to get this nightmare to stop was to confess."

Peterson, a lifelong police officer, must have been well aware of how seldom the missing are found in the environs of Bolingbrook and how incredibly unlikely it would be for local prosecutors to bring a murder charge without a body or clear indication that a crime had been committed. Peterson's knowledge of the Fox ordeal and resulting lawsuit—a huge source of rancor among the Will County police community—would make local detectives and prosecutors hesitant to risk another of its kind.

Then again, as one veteran deputy with the sheriff's department that investigated Riley Fox's death suggested, maybe Peterson was just looking for a way to get rich quick.

"What if," the deputy speculated to me, "he saw this Fox mess, and he said to his wife, 'Honey, take the bus to Wyoming and check into a hotel and do not call anybody. Pay for everything in cash and stay there and wait for me to get a hold of you.'

"He has to know, with his history, with the last wife and everything, they're going to be looking at him," the cop said. "So he starts acting all goofy and he goes on TV and says stupid shit. And then when they arrest him, his wife shows up and he sues the county."

There's no evidence whatsoever that this was Peterson's plan. If it was, he has yet to pull off the part where he gets the police to arrest him, at least for anything more substantial than an unrelated weapons charge. Stacy might have to stay in that Wyoming hotel room for an awfully long time.

CHAPTER SIX

After so much upheaval in a short period of time—his romance with Stacy, his explosive split and subsequent feud with Savio, followed by her untimely and strange death—Drew Peterson must have looked forward to the spring and summer of 2004 to bring a measure of peace to his life. The ex-wife up the street who had given him all that grief was gone. Remarkably, a state police investigation into her death found nothing untoward, and a coroner's jury had ruled the cause to be accidental drowning, taking the heat of suspicion off of her ex-husband.

In the relative calm, the Petersons could conceivably turn their attention to their still-new marriage and focus on their now considerable parenting duties. Their son, Anthony, who had been born in July 2003, was hitting all the milestones that delight parents as children approach their first birthdays, and Stacy was pregnant with their second child, daughter Lacy. Additionally, the couple now shared their home with Kristopher and Thomas, the two sons of Drew Peterson and Kathleen Savio, who went to live with their father after their mother died.

Adding to the crowd at 6 Pheasant Chase Court was Stephen Peterson, Drew's adult son from his first marriage, and Stephen's girlfriend, a young woman named Jennifer. Both were college students at the time, living in the Peterson basement.

And the Peterson clan was about to meet new next-door neighbors, Sharon and Bob Bychowski, who had just moved to Pheasant Chase Court.

Despite the twenty-six-year difference in their ages, Stacy and Bychowski immediately bonded the day in April 2004 when Stacy, with much of her famly in tow, walked over to introduce everyone.

"She was your friend in five minutes and your best friend in ten," Sharon Bychowski recalled. "Family and friendships were so important to her."

Bychowski saw a lot of herself in the young woman. Like Stacy, she had been a young mother—her son Roy was born when she was seventeen—and had taken up with a much older man, but the relationship didn't last. At nineteen, she struck out on her own selling Avon products; at twenty-five, she was hired as a manager. She eventually met Bob Bychowski, to whom she'd been married for twenty-two years when Stacy's disappearance turned her life upside down. By the time she moved next door to Stacy she had become an Avon district manager with her own secretary.

For the next three and a half years, until Stacy vanished, Stacy and Bychowski regularly dropped by each other's homes and Bychowski, by her own account, became close with the family, often watching the kids, giving them treats, and listening to Stacy when she needed to unload the growing stress in her marriage.

That April day they met, only about a month and a half after Savio died, Bychowski had no idea of the recent turmoil in her new neighborhood. She would soon learn. About six weeks after moving in, Bychowski recalled, while talking with Stacy over the back fence, Peterson ambled over and said, "You know, my last wife died."

Bychowski was so taken aback she could only laugh in astonishment.

"I'm like, 'Okay, are you serious?' And he goes, 'Oh yeah, yeah. It was ruled an accident. That was close.'"

Stacy then asked Bychowski if she wanted to go down and look at Savio's house, which they were cleaning to sell. Bychowski, who loves looking at homes for sale, agreed. It was on this trip that Stacy divulged how she and Drew used to have sex in the basement of that house while the rest of the family slept upstairs.

According to Bychowski, Stacy took her neighbor into her confidence many times after that. Those heady nights in the basement seemed long gone as Stacy opened up to the older woman about the couple's ever more frequent fights, which sometimes grew violent, and of Stacy's growing determination to leave her husband. If Drew Peterson had in fact found some peace in the spring and summer of 2004, it didn't last.

Bychowski said she could tell right away the honeymoon was over at 6 Pheasant Chase Court, unless the honeymoon involved physical blows. If anything, she said, the couple mellowed over time and the fights became less fierce.

"When I first moved here, they were more physical," Bychowski said. "But, see, she would hit him back. So stuff started breaking in the house. Then he realized she's going to hit me back and it's going to spin out of control. So he started following her."

His "following" was often done by cell phone. "Everywhere we went—Kohl's, to get a haircut, to pick up my granddaughter—he always called," Bychowski described. "At first I think she thought it was nice, but as it went on...."

Peterson denies ever raising a hand to his wife and says that, if anything, he was on the receiving end of any battering. For a time, he repeated an oft-broadcast story of Stacy striking him in the head with a frozen steak. He said she "hated being cornered" but maintains he never hit her. Peterson also points out that he has never been charged in connection with a domestic incident, much less had the police called to his home for a problem with Stacy. While he and Savio were frequent subjects in police reports, there were never any such reports involving him and his fourth wife.

Relatives of Stacy, particularly her "stepsister" Kerry Simmons, who is actually a half sister of a half sister and not a blood relative at all, told a different story. Simmons said on the *Dateline* NBC show which aired on

December 22 that Peterson "threw [Stacy] down the stairs. There was an instance where he had knocked her into the TV. I think one time he actually picked her up and threw her across the room. I mean, she's small. She's a hundred pounds."

Bychowski said she would walk away when she saw or heard the couple fighting. "I mean, that's not my place." Stacy, she said, "was willing to sort out everything herself."

Stacy may have insisted she was able to handle her husband on her own, but Bychowski also recalls the young woman expressing her fear of being unable to escape a horrible fate, even predicting her impending death.

"She would just constantly say to me, 'If I'm missing it's not an accident. He killed me,'" Bychowski said. "She would say it to me all the time. Many, many, many times."

So what were Drew and Stacy fighting about? No outsider can know for sure what happens within a marriage, but based on the accounts of friends and family, certain issues were likely sources of conflict. One was Drew's jealousy, his suspicion that Stacy was sneaking around with other men; the three-decade difference in their ages may have ceased to be a novelty.

On her end, Stacy went from being a single seventeen-year-old to a mother of four in less than three years. While by all accounts she was a devoted mother, even to the children who weren't hers biologically—Bychowski recalled Stacy helping Kristopher with his math homework and throwing parties in Thomas' honor—raising four children is a huge responsibility that could easily put stress on a marriage.

One event that inarguably took an emotional toll on Stacy was the death of her half sister, Tina Ryan. Tina succumbed to colon cancer in September of 2006, at the age of thirty-one, and Stacy was devastated. Soon afterward, Peterson said, his wife became depressed and lost her faith in God. She set up what Peterson called a "shrine" to Tina on a bookshelf in the corner of Peterson's office, to the side of his large wooden desk. He showed it to me after Stacy disappeared. The shelves contained pictures of Tina, as well as various knickknacks and mementos that seemed based on a Disney theme. As time marched on with no sign of Stacy, the number of artifacts in the shrine dwindled, which to Peterson was just as well: "It gives me more room for my own things." While Stacy must have tried to find solace in the objects during the numb days following her half sister's death, the items apparently did not hold the same sentimental value for Peterson.

At one time the shrine included an urn holding Tina's ashes, but, in one of the odder episodes of the Stacy Peterson story, close to two weeks after she was reported missing, her husband returned the remains to Tina's family while Geraldo Rivera was broadcasting live from the Bychowskis' house. A few members of the family stepped over to Peterson's house to collect the ashes while Rivera tried without success to get the relatives to agree that a potential hostage situation could be developing inside 6 Pheasant Chase Court. These ashes were just one of the few mementos Stacy had to remember Tina by.

Peterson's former friend, Ric Mims, even said on a television interview with Fox News' Greta Van Susteren that Stacy was taking mood-altering drugs to help her deal with her grief over the death of Tina, which may have further affected her emotional state. Bychowski remembered watching in shock as Mims made his statements for the camera right in her own home, which she had allowed to be used for the taping.

"Ric was going on and on about how she was under psychiatric care," Bychowski said. "And I'm looking at him like, 'Oh, my God, what do I do? Do I jump up and say this is really ridiculous, stop taping, get out?'"

Bychowski said Stacy wasn't "psychiatric nuts." She did take Prozac after having her babies because "she had a terrible time with postpartum depression," Bychowski said, but she didn't stay on the drug because it made her tired, and the medication conflicted with allergy medicine she took.

Stacy might not have been "psychiatric nuts," but Peterson blamed the effect Tina's death had on her for the "emotional roller coaster" that life with his wife had turned into. (At other times, he blamed her menstrual cycle.) Then again, he'd described life with Savio in the same terms. Peterson's last two marriages apparently were a veritable amusement park of emotion.

"She [Savio] came from an abusive home-life growing up. She had abusive stepparents," Peterson told Matt Lauer during an interview on the *Today* show. "At first it was very romantic and, again, after she had children, hormones kicked in and, again, an emotional roller coaster with her."

He seemed to feel more pity for himself than for either of his last two wives, with their less than ideal upbringings, or, for that matter, the deceased Tina Ryan. Whatever sorrow he felt over his dead half sister-in-law he kept very well hidden, indeed. For example, instead of helping his wife get through the difficult day of Tina's funeral, the event instead brought out Peterson's jealousy.

Tina's wake and funeral were held in the small town of Marseilles, Illinois, and both Peterson and his neighbor Bychowski said numerous friends and relatives attended. Stacy described the services as heart-wrenching, Bychowski said. Stacy and Tina's husband, Jamie, were particularly overcome.

The day after the funeral, Bychowski said, when Stacy came next door to visit, she wasn't herself. Bychowski, who had also lost a sister to cancer, told Stacy she understood how hard it was when a loved one died.

"So she said to me, 'That's not really my problem,'" Bychowski recalled. Stacy told her that she and Drew had had a big fight at the funeral. Stacy, her father, her sister Cassandra, Jamie, and Drew were all standing around the casket, saying goodbye. The others walked off after their farewells, but Stacy and Jamie stayed. "And she said, 'I just couldn't tear myself away. It was very hard to say goodbye for the last time.'

"She said to Jamie, 'Let's just do it together. Let's just walk away together.' So they turned at the same time and they walked outside, and when they walked into the hallway, Drew said to her, 'Are you fucking Jamie?'

"My God, she was absolutely devastated by that."

They argued in the car on the way home, Bychowski said, and he kept up the argument into the night. "He used to do that a lot," she said. "He would keep her sleep deprived and argue with her all night long and not let her sleep."

Bychowski said Stacy simply could not believe he would accuse her, right at Tina's funeral, of sleeping with her half sister's husband. That was, in Bychowski's mind, when Stacy made the decision that she would be better off if she was no longer married to her husband.

"She was so devastated, is the only word I could use, and hurt and upset by that. She said, 'I've got to make some changes. I've got to do something different. I've got to divorce him.'"

Stacy's aunt Candace also claims Stacy wanted to part with Peterson. She was considering a move to either Phoenix or somewhere in California, Aikin said.

"She told me when I was there [visiting in October, 2007] she was trying to find a way to get out and take the children."

And by "the children," Candace Aikin said, Stacy did not just mean the two she had given birth to, Anthony and Lacy. She planned on taking along the sons of Kathleen Savio, Kristopher and Thomas, when she escaped from Drew Peterson.

Peterson himself, in the last months before Stacy disappeared, also wanted the family to move—but not without him. Bychowski said the couple first visited Arizona, with the idea that it would be close to Stacy's aunt in California. Then they looked at property in California, Bychowski said, but found nothing in their price range.

In the summer of 2007, Drew's new idea was Kentucky and possibly bringing Stacy's dad along to live nearby. But Stacy told Bychowski there was no way that would happen.

"Stacy hates Kentucky," Aikin seconded. "Stacy wouldn't live in Kentucky."

Strangely enough, after Stacy disappeared, Peterson's attorney, Joel Brodsky, released an anonymous letter that put Stacy in the parking lot of a shopping mall in

Folorence, Kentucky, on November 18, 2007. She was in the company of an unidentified man. The letter was sent to Peterson's Bolingbrook home but was addressed to "Joel Peterson."

The letter writer claims that when she approached Stacy, the woman implored her to leave her alone: "Please don't ruin my life. Please. I just want to be left alone, please." Stacy then supposedly hotfooted it away, but not before the quick-witted anonymous-letter writer captured her image by snapping a cell phone photograph. Disappointingly, no photograph was enclosed with the letter.

Peterson had taken a road trip with his children to Disney World about the time the letter would have been mailed—he found it in his mailbox the day he got back. The letter was postmarked in Cincinnati, Ohio, which would have been on the likely route from Bolingbrook to Orlando, Florida. Brodsky insisted his client and children did not go that way while on the road to the Magic Kingdom.

Aikin, Bychowski, and Pamela Bosco, the legal guardian of Stacy's little sister, Cassandra Cales, all dismissed the possible validity of anonymous letters.

There is no evidence that Stacy ever got away, but even if she had, both Aikin and Bychowski are sure it would not have been to Kentucky and most certainly not to the part where Drew took her father to visit, a region Bychowski claims did not even boast a Wal-Mart.

Even though Stacy's aunt and father figured into the relocation plans at various points, in Bychowski's view Peterson sought to move in order to isolate Stacy from her family: "Control people do that," she said.

Bychowski clearly saw a control motive in much that transpired between Peterson and his wife. His need for control manifested itself, she said, in his reaction to Minnie, a miniature pinscher that Stacy's sister, Cassandra, had given her. The puppy did not last long in the Peterson household. Drew forced her to get rid of it, Bychowski said, because he hated that it peed in the house.

Peterson disputed this version of events. He said that he and Stacy agreed to get rid of the dog—she gave it to a coworker of her father's—because it was not housebroken and no one took the time to train it. To Bychowski, however, the dog was just an example of Peterson getting his way and of Stacy following his direction.

Bychowski and Peterson also took different views of Stacy's motivation to embark, in August of 2006, on an extensive self-improvement program.

Stacy gave birth to the couple's first child, Anthony, in July of 2003. A year and a half later, nineteen days before Stacy's twenty-first birthday, came the second baby, Lacy, named after Stacy's sister who died as an infant. Stacy was of course still young—not even old enough to legally buy liquor by the time she had her second child—but after giving birth to two kids in eighteen months, her body was not the same. She decided to make some changes.

She began with breast augmentation, braces, and Lasik eye surgery so she would not have to wear glasses. The coup de grâce for the 2006 upgrade plan was, as her husband termed it, "hair removal."

While Stacy agreed to the procedures, and may have even asked for them, the extent of the breast augmentation was a point of contention between husband and wife, Bychowski said.

"She was an A [cup] and then she breast-fed her two kids," she said. "So she went to a C. He wanted her to go to a double D; what an asshole. And the doctor said, 'Absolutely not. Her frame will not carry that big of breasts. She'll be uncomfortable. She'll have back issues. I will not do that. I'll take her to a C and that's it.' So that's what she had. She thought that was realistic. But he wanted her to go up to a double D. It's a big joke for him."

The overhaul continued into the next year. About two months before she vanished, Stacy underwent painful liposuction on her legs along with what Bychowski described as an excruciating tummy tuck.

"She was a hundred thirty [pounds] before surgery," Bychowski said. "Then she had liposuction on her legs. I said to her, 'Where?' And then she had the tummy tuck."

It was the tummy tuck, or abdominoplasty, that Bychowski said was the real killer. During abdominoplasty, excess skin and fat in the abdominal area are surgically removed and the muscles tightened. There are numerous risks associated with the surgery, and Stacy's recovery was a long and agonizing one.

"When she had her tummy tuck, she was on the floor in the living room. Nobody could touch her," Bychowski said. "She had drains in her for like four days. She was on the floor because she couldn't get up. She was on a mattress in the living room so she could be a part of the family still. Then they took out her drains and then she still couldn't hardly walk. It's like major surgery."

The surgery left a "hairline" scar that wouldn't show when she wore a bikini, Bychowski said. "But it looked odd. It looked like they recreated her belly button. Which they did."

On the bright side, the scar was partially covered by one of Stacy's two tattoos: red cherries with green leaves inked across her right-front hip. She also had a blue-and-yellow carnation on the small of her back.

In Bychowski's view, her friend's "improved" form was a little much. "It looked weird, you know, when she was in her bathing suit," Bychowski said. "She's totally like a big, giant hourglass."

Of course, to the person having all that surgery, and the person paying for it, an hourglass figure might have been precisely the desired outcome. In Peterson's mind, he'd gallantly accommodated his wife's desire to enhance her appearance. He viewed himself in general as an overindulgent husband, pampering his young wife after her hardscrabble upbringing. The surgeries and physical renovations lay on the same continuum as the apartment, furniture, Grand Prix and other gifts that he'd showered on his teenage girlfriend when their love was new. As Peterson said on *Dateline* NBC, "Stacy wanted [it], she got it.

"I mean, she wanted a boob job, I got her a boob job," he said. "She wanted a tummy tuck, she got that. She wanted braces, Lasik surgery, hair removal, anything.

"Stacy loved male attention," her husband explained. "And she loved being anywhere and having people pay attention to her."

Still, Bychowski had no doubt that Peterson was trying to mold his wife into his ideal of a woman, and Stacy was susceptible to his opinions.

"He was trying to make her into what he wanted," she said. "Absolutely. I think she really wanted to be as good as she could be. If somebody tells you you're fat, somebody tells you, 'God, you've got a lot of stretch marks, you're just not the person I married,' what do you do? You've got to make a choice. You either try to get better or you give up. I don't think she wanted to give up."

Perhaps not when she began her self-improvement regimen, but in the three and a half years Stacy had been her friend, Bychowski had seen quite a change—physical and otherwise—in the young mother who had trotted her family over to meet the new neighbor in April 2004.

One member of that day's parade was no longer living as part of the family by the time Stacy disappeared: Jennifer, the then-girlfriend of Stephen Peterson, who had been living in the basement. According to Bychowski, Jennifer left for quite a valid reason:

"Jennifer came home to find Steve screwing someone in the basement," she said. "So she packed her things and went back home."

Bychowski said Stacy loved the young woman and felt terrible about what had supposedly happened. At the same time, the echoes of Stacy's own basement trysting with Peterson in the early days of their clandestine affair were not lost on her.

"Know what she said to me?" Bychowski said. "'Like father, like son.'"

CHAPTER SEVEN

The number of jobs that Drew Peterson has held rivals the number of women he's romanced. Just as Peterson usually didn't confine himself to the woman to whom he was married, his career as a police officer, while the basis of his professional identity, wasn't the only work that occupied him.

"I've had six jobs at one time," said Peterson, ticking off such trades as running printing and prepress businesses, owning a chimney-sweeping service, dabbling in wedding photography, getting involved with his former pal Ric Mims in cable-television installation, having a share in a karate school, and presiding over his tavern, Suds Pub, in the town of Montgomery, Illinois, about seventeen miles west of Bolingbrook.

Peterson could juggle the day jobs because his police work took place on the overnight shift. This allowed him to keep business hours for himself. He made a lot of money, he said, but the schedule was exhausting.

To be sure, Drew Peterson loved the good life that his many jobs afforded, so it was probably fortunate that he'd put in all those hours and socked away some money. The roughly $6,000-a-month police pension that he began collecting after his retirement in December of 2007, while hardly chump change, wasn't going to maintain the lifestyle to which he'd become accustomed. Also, since his fourth wife's disappearance, he faced the additional burden of legal fees. These concerned him enough that shortly after he retired he set up a Web site, DefendDrew.com, that accepted donations through PayPal to foot his legal bills and fund the search for Stacy, with any leftover dollars going into trust for his children. The site attracted so much traffic that the host company shut it down within a day. Peterson's attorney, Joel Brodsky, said the site was closed because it had achieved the short-term goals they'd set. That said, he refuses to reveal how much money the site actually took in.

But a love of money was not the only motive Peterson had for pursuing so many professions. In his heyday, before his recent troubles, Peterson was even something of a Renaissance man. As a police officer, he cut a figure of uniformed authority. With a hand in the bar business, he assumed the role of publican. He was an expert in the martial and the photographic arts, running the karate school and the wedding-picture business. If that weren't enough, Peterson was a motorcycle enthusiast who purchased a thirty-thousand-dollar bike after he turned fifty. He is also a licensed pilot with his very own airplane.

Peterson said he flew general-aviation airplanes when he was younger, having earned his license when he was seventeen. At the time Stacy vanished he was the proud owner of an Aquilla Trike, worth about twenty grand. The open-sided, two-seater, microlight craft barely resembles a plane at all, instead looking more like a three-wheeled jogging stroller with a propeller mounted in back, the entire contraption dangling from a hang glider. Peterson had his Aquilla imported from South Africa, where the trikes are made, and kept it in a hangar at Cushing Field in Newark, Illinois, about thirty miles from his Bolingbrook home. In a conversation with me he said he had a good story about his ordeal in getting the Aquilla to the United States from South Africa, but never elaborated.

Peterson did not short himself on toys. Besides the motorcycle and airplane, he had a camper, a swimming pool, at least eleven guns, two cars, and a couple of computers. He also lived in a spacious, two-story home with a vaulted living room ceiling; and after his daughter, Lacy, was born in 2005, Peterson had four children under the age of twelve to take care of, as well as a wife who, in the eighteen months before she vanished, racked up five-figure bills for a comprehensive cosmetic overhaul. Shorting himself on women no less than on toys, Peterson had also weathered three divorces that certainly set him back monetarily, although his financial settlement with Savio was never finalized before she died.

While he appeared to have been a profligate spender, Peterson must have also been a saver—if his reported claims that his young wife snatched twenty-five thousand dollars in cash right before she disappeared are to be believed.

Bank records show, however, that after Stacy vanished Peterson sent more than ten times that much to his son Stephen, one of the two adult stepsons nineteen-year-old Stacy had acquired in her marriage to Drew.

Peterson wrote several checks to the twenty-eight-year-old, who followed in his father's footsteps to become a police officer in nearby Oak Brook, Illinois. Reportedly, one of the checks was in excess of one hundred and fifty thousand dollars, and some were from joint accounts in the names of both Stacy and Drew Peterson. Peterson later explained to me the good sense behind this innocent action: he was merely trying to prevent Stacy from looting the bank accounts herself from a remote location.

Peterson was lucky to have that kind of cash on hand, with the prospect of funding a pricey and lengthy legal battle in connection not only with Stacy's disappearance but the death of his third wife, now officially a homicide, looming over his head. Because he was a suspect in the "potential homicide" of his missing wife, the dread of going to jail gnawed at Peterson. He compared it to having cancer, to waking up every day facing a truly frightening future.

That was the introspective Drew Peterson. The artistic Drew Peterson photographed and captured wedding memories for marrying couples and engaged in kung fu fighting. Of course, he was a lover, as well; a man who seemingly was never going to restrict himself to one woman for life, as evidenced by his four marriages and the extramarital affairs he freely admits to.

It's difficult to imagine Peterson finding time for so many business ventures, so many children—he fathered six and had one stepdaughter—and so many women. But by his own account, and those of some of his ex-wives, he did. Peterson talked to me briefly about one "girlfriend" he had while he was married to his second wife. He was adamant about not having anything to do with the apparent suicide of her brother, who was found hanging in his garage, but as far as sleeping with the woman while he was married to someone else—yeah, Peterson said, that happened.

Peterson spread himself around, it seemed, in all aspects of his life. "At one time, I employed over a hundred people," Peterson told me, and among those on his payroll were relatives and in-laws, people he said he was "supporting." In fact, he couldn't seem to help collecting people who needed support and who, in contrast to Peterson's police-officer duty to uphold law and order, didn't exactly stick to the straight and narrow. There was, for example, his second wife's motorcycle-gangster brother who got shot to death, and Stacy's brother, Yelton, a registered sex offender.

One in-law Peterson gave a job to was Savio's nephew, Charlie Doman. Doman first worked as a maintenance man at Suds Pub, owned jointly by his Aunt Kitty and her then-husband, Peterson. From there, he moved into the kitchen, and was then made a manager.

"Then my Aunt Kitty fired me," Doman recalled.

But they apparently ironed out their difficulties, because Savio and Peterson brought Doman back to Suds Pub to work as a DJ.

After he left the bar, however, Doman ran into some trouble of his own. He pleaded guilty to felony aggravated battery in connection with an August 1998 stabbing. He stuck a knife in a sleeping "friend" numerous times and was charged with attempted murder on top of the aggravated battery.

Doman's friend survived the attack, and Doman's ensuing plea deal got him off with probation and the two hundred twenty-three days he'd spent in jail awaiting trial.

In 2003, Doman landed back behind bars after pleading guilty to a theft charge. He supposedly walked off with his boss' cash register and the money it held. The judge gave him two years.

Doman said that was a "different time" in his life, and he's settled down since. But before he went to prison, before he even stabbed his friend, he worked in his brother-in-law's bar in various capacities. While there, he made the acquaintance of Drew's stepbrother, Tom Morphey, another relative to whom Peterson gave a helping hand.

Peterson and Morphey became stepbrothers in adulthood, after Peterson's father and Morphey's mother had died, and the surviving parents got married. Peterson's father, Donald Peterson, had worked for Morphey's father at the Northern Illinois Gas Company. Peterson said his father was diagnosed with cancer immediately after he retired.

"That's some way to spend your retirement," he said.

Peterson said that it was at his father's funeral, in fact, that his mother met Al Morphey, her future husband, whose wife had also died from cancer. Thus did Drew Peterson and Tom Morphey become family, forming a bond that, according to at least one police source, eventually led to police linking the pair in a diabolical deed that may yet turn out to be more fact than fiction.

Tom Morphey was nowhere nearly as successful as his gas-company-executive father. He reputedly struggled with addiction and was twice convicted of drunken driving. A former girlfriend twice sought to obtain protective orders, accusing Morphey of leaving on her answering machine a message that said, "Watch your back. Don't go to sleep. You'll be taken care of."

Morphey was also arrested for domestic violence. He pleaded guilty in exchange for court supervision but saw the supervision revoked when he failed to submit to psychological evaluation.

Morphey had made a mess of his life, but gregarious Drew Peterson threw him a lifeline by giving him a job at Suds Pub.

Charlie Doman said Morphey not only drank at work, but was also known to pass out on the job, becoming inebriated well before closing time. Still, Doman said, "He was a real nice, honest guy."

A nice, honest guy, albeit one with some personal troubles. Yet if Morphey's friend Walter Martineck's public pronouncements are to be believed, Morphey would one day be involved in an entirely different kind of trouble with Peterson.

Martineck and Morphey both lived on Thistle Drive in Bolingbrook, about a mile or so from Drew Peterson. Coincidentally, Charlie Doman once lived on Thistle Drive too, as did his mother, Anna Marie, and sister, Melissa. They had relocated to Romeoville by the time Stacy Peterson vanished. Charlie and Anna Marie Doman say they did not know Martineck and that Morphey did not live on the street when they did.

But Morphey was there at the end of October 2007, and on November 30, just more than a month after Stacy was last seen alive, Martineck went on the *Today* show to talk about his neighbor down the street.

Martineck explained that he and Morphey, then forty, had been friends for years. On *Today*, Martineck said his old pal had told him that Peterson paid him money to help him move a large container the same day Stacy disappeared. Morphey supposedly assisted Peterson in moving this container from his second-story bedroom to his GMC Denali outside.

"He was real frantic. I could tell he'd been drinking a little," Martineck said of his meeting with Morphey. "He put his hands on my shoulders and says, 'You can't tell no one. I know she was in there.'"

Morphey then tried to give him the money Peterson paid him, Martineck said, but he would not take it and doesn't know how much it was.

The day after Stacy disappeared, Morphey tried to kill himself because "he was just afraid of his family's life," Martineck said. Afraid for his family's life, perhaps, envisioning the aftermath of whatever Drew Peterson had drawn him into. Bolingbrook Fire Department logs show an 11 p.m., October 29, report of Morphey overdosing on sleeping pills.

An interview with Martineck later aired on the prime-time news program *Dateline* NBC. On this show, he said Morphey told him, "I went with Drew to his house. He asked me to help him move something, and I said, 'Yeah.'

"I go, 'That's understood, but what do you mean, Stacy?'" Martineck said. "And he goes, 'Well, we lifted a blue container out of—out of his room down into his truck.' 'Well, how do you know it's Stacy?' 'It was warm.' And the way he said 'warm,' it's like it was warm."

Martineck says Peterson even provided Morphey with a motive.

"Because, like, from what Tom said, Stacy was filing for a divorce," he explained. "And Drew had to be out and apparently Drew wanted everything to himself."

When questioned about his statements on network television, Martineck refused to elaborate.

After Morphey overdosed on pills and alcohol and was taken to the hospital, he received a visit from his brother-in-law.

"Yeah, I went to see him in the hospital," Peterson recalled. "I think it was the next day."

From the hospital, Morphey went somewhere that wasn't his home.

His live-in girlfriend, Sheryl Alcox, told the *Chicago Sun-Times* a month after Stacy had vanished that Morphey had not been home in "several" weeks.

"He's in therapy," Alcox explained, and in the months that followed, he was nowhere to be found on Thistle Drive.

If Martineck's story about Morphey believing he unwittingly helped carry a container holding Stacy's body was anywhere close to being on the money, the man's conscience must have been consuming him. But then various media outlets reported stories about Morphey doing much more than helping carry a container. If true, Morphey no longer seemed quite so unwitting.

Peterson dismissed all of it: from his paying off Morphey to help him get rid of Stacy, to the very existence of the blue barrel he supposedly carted out of his home the night Stacy was last seen.

"He was one of those guys who was needy all the time, like Mims," Peterson said of Morphey, comparing his stepbrother to Ric Mims, the former friend and fellow cable-television installer who had bunkered down with Peterson and his children in their home in the first few days after Stacy's disappearance, but then turned on his old pal, selling a scurrilous story to the *National Enquirer*, reportedly for thousands of dollars.

"I helped him out," Peterson said of Morphey, sounding, as he did immediately after Stacy disappeared, like a grieved, betrayed benefactor. "I gave him furniture." At the time Stacy disappeared, he was also trying to line up a job for Morphey at the local Meijer department store.

"To know him is to love him, because he's such an idiot," Peterson has said of his stepbrother.

"He's a nice lovable guy," Peterson said, "but he's fucked up all the time."

Morphey paid back this kindness, if Martineck is to be believed, by shooting his mouth off and all but accusing Peterson of killing his wife, stuffing her in a barrel, and sneaking her body out of the house.

"The guy definitely had mental problems," Peterson said of his stepbrother. He has his own theory on what may have been motivating Martineck and Morphey. It was the same thing he said was motivating Mims.

"Maybe those guys were trying to get their fifteen minutes of fame," he said.

Someone was lying, that much was clear, but was it Peterson, in his denials of moving a barrel with his stepbrother? Or was it Martineck, telling a big story in front of the television cameras? Or could it have been

Morphey himself, heading over to Martineck's door and spinning a yarn either out of a need for attention or due to something rooted in illness or delusion?

If Morphey has made it back to Thistle Drive since he was taken to the hospital at the end of October, he has not been venturing outside or answering the door. He was rumored to be in some sort of police-protected custody until he could be used to testify before the grand jury investigating the death of Kathleen Savio and disappearance of Stacy Peterson.

But his value as a witness was questionable, at least according to one police source.

The state's attorney's office was reluctant to put Morphey in front of the grand jury for fear his testimony would not amount to much, the source said. When it came to the night in question, Morphey was afflicted with "memory lapses," the source said, and his recollection of helping his stepbrother carry a barrel out to the waiting GMC Denali was less than lucid.

In the months following Stacy's disappearance, Peterson said he had not heard from his stepbrother and did not know where he had gone. In the spring of 2008, Peterson claimed he knew exactly where Morphey was: "The police are sitting on him, not to protect him; the police are sitting on him to clean him up."

Still Peterson conceded he did not actually have any idea where it was that the police may have been "sitting" on his stepbrother.

Besides, Peterson had far greater concerns—the police executing search warrant after search warrant at his home and the weekly grand jury hearings to which his family and friends were called to testify, not to mention a felony weapons charge hanging over his head—than Tom Morphey's whereabouts. At one time, not too long ago, Peterson said he was trying to get his stepbrother a job. Now he did not even know how to find him.

But jobs—for his stepbrother or, after so many years of burning the candle at both ends, for himself—were the last thing on Peterson's mind. He had just retired from the one he'd worked at for twenty-nine years, and he did not miss it a bit.

"Am I missing it? Not really," Peterson said in regards to his mental state after walking away from his life as a police officer. "I have too much other stuff on my plate to worry about anything."

And the man who worked six jobs at a time, who once had more than a hundred people on his payroll, had no strong desire to pursue gainful employment. A new job was out of the question. With his young wife missing and the police looking at him as the primary suspect, so was his love life.

"I'm not going to get another date," he said.

Not if his next-door neighbor Sharon Bychowski has anything to do with it. Ever since Stacy went missing, Bychowski has spearheaded efforts to search for her and keep her memory alive. She's also vowed to tell any young woman seen venturing into Peterson's home exactly what she suspects happened to his last wife, not to mention the one before her.

"He'll never have a girlfriend out here that I won't say something to," Bychowski said.

What will Bychowski tell the next prospective Peterson love interest?

"You need to think about this. The last one died. The one before that died. You're next."

Stacy Peterson (right), the fourth wife of Bolingbrook Police Sergeant Drew Peterson, appears naked underneath an oversized blazer. Her sister, Cassandra Cales, is decked out in Drew's SWAT team regalia and is toting his AR-15, the semi-automatic assault rifle that would land him in jail on a felony weapons charge in May of 2008. Asked if he was the one who shot the picture, Peterson, a professional wedding photographer, said, "No comment."

The home of Drew and Stacy Peterson, where the couple lived with their two children, Anthony and Lacy, as well as the two born to Peterson's third wife, Kathleen Savio. The house, on a quiet Bolingbrook cul-de-sac, was under media siege for months after Stacy disappeared.
Photo credit: Joseph Hosey

The home of Drew Peterson and Kathleen Savio. Peterson trysted with his girlfriend Stacy in the basement of this house. When Kathleen realized he was cheating, she kicked him out and he moved down the street. She would be found drowned in her dry bathtub soon after.
Photo credit: Joseph Hosey

Stacy Peterson, the seventeen-year-old bride of Drew Peterson, who bore the disgraced police officer a pair of children before vanishing without a trace three days before Halloween 2007.

Drew Peterson drapes his arm around Stacy, his fourth wife.

Stacy's older brother, convict and registered sex offender Yelton Cales, was doing time in a western Illinois prison when his sister disappeared.
Photo credit: Illinois State Police

Kathleen Savio, pictured here on the day of her wedding with Drew Peterson, wound up drowned in a dry bathtub in the midst of their contentious divorce.

LOVING MOTHER & SISTER
KATHLEEN SAVIO
JUNE 13, 1963 – MAR. 1, 2004
ALWAYS IN OUR HEARTS

The grave of Kathleen Savio in Hillside's Queen of Heaven Cemetery. Savio's eternal resting place was disturbed when authorities dug up her body for additional postmortem testing in the wake of Stacy's disappearance. Photo credit: Janet Lundquist

Candace Aikin, known to Stacy and her siblings as Aunt Candy, told a grand jury about her niece's relationship with husband Drew Peterson.

Sharon Bychowski was Stacy's next-door neighbor and best friend. She spearheaded the search efforts for the missing mother and the drive to keep media attention focused on the case.
Photo credit: Joseph Hosey

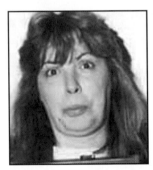

Christie Marie Toutges Cales, the mother of Stacy Peterson, shown here in a Westmont, Illinois, Police Department mug shot. Christie's life was one of sorrow and reported alcoholism. She herself vanished in March of 1998. Photo credit: Westmont Police Department

Sharon Bychowski fueled tensions between herself and Drew Peterson when she placed this sign in her front yard. The sign migrated to other homes around the cul-de-sac before returning to Bychowski's, where it was surrounded by flowers and other mementos. Photo credit: Joseph Hosey

Drew Peterson's former fiancée, Kyle Piry, testified in front of a special grand jury convened to review the death of Kathleen Savio and the disappearance of Stacy Peterson. Piry and Peterson were briefly engaged to marry in the early 1980s; both claim to have called an end to the romance.

Walter Martineck, longtime friend of Drew Peterson's stepbrother, Thomas Morphey, grabs a smoke prior to testifying before the grand jury.

Drew Peterson surveys tire tracks in his cul-de-sac. He accused his sister-in-law, Cassandra Cales, of laying down the rubber in an attempt to harass and annoy him.

Will County State's Attorney James Glasgow and his spokesman, Charles B. Pelkie, stand for the camera. Glasgow handled the investigation into Stacy's disappearance and Kathleen's death.

Anna Marie Doman, sister of Drew Peterson's slain third wife, Kathleen, endures a crush of media as she exits after a grand jury appearance in May of 2008.

Stacy's father, Anthony Cales, walks into the county-owned building where the special grand jury reviewing his daughter's disappearance has been convened. Cales has claimed to know little, if anything, of the circumstances surrounding Stacy's disappearance, and said he wondered why prosecutors bothered calling him.

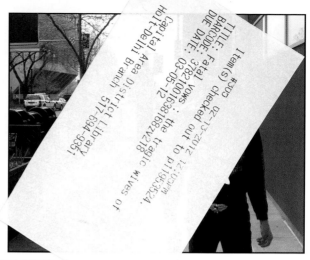

Drew Peterson in spring 2008, just moments after explaining that he may or may not be dating a twenty-two-year-old woman working the desk at a local tanning salon.

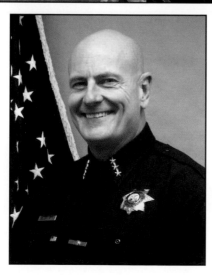

Chief Ray McGury inherited Drew Peterson when he took the job to head up the Bolingbrook Police Department. Overnight Sergeant Peterson may have made his boss wish he had stayed in Naperville.
Photo credit: Bolingbrook Police Chief Ray McGury

Searchers examine a soiled bed sheet while on the hunt for any sign of Stacy Peterson. The discovery led to brief excitement, and search organizers forbade photographers to take pictures or film the event, but ultimately nothing came of it.
Photo credit: Joseph Hosey

Roy Taylor, the son of Sharon Bychowski, leads a volunteer search operation. As the search coordinator, Taylor worked closely with the Illinois State Police.
Photo credit: Joseph Hosey

CHAPTER EIGHT

By mid-2006, the once-torrid February-October romance of the teenage hotel desk clerk and the middle-age suburban cop had mellowed into marriage and parenthood. After Stacy's half sister Tina Ryan died in September of 2006, things took a decided turn for the worse, and by the autumn of 2007, the relationship between Drew and Stacy Peterson was nothing short of rocky.

Stacy's grief over her half sister's death understandably put stress on the Petersons' marriage, but Drew Peterson actually blamed the couple's misery on his wife's menstrual cycle. Whenever she got her period, she wanted a divorce and then settled down again when it had passed, he claimed. Others say Stacy, period or no period, was on her way out by early October 2007, if not sooner.

What's not debatable is that ever since Stacy was last seen on October 28, 2007, several people have come forward—either through the media or the grand jury investigating her disappearance—to speak to Stacy's activities and state of mind in the weeks before she vanished.

Candace Aikin said Stacy told her she was getting ready to leave her husband, an announcement that almost forced Aikin to alter a visit to Illinois where she planned to attend a nephew's birthday party in October of 2007. She was going to stay in Bolingbrook with the Petersons, as she usually did.

"I was out there a lot, and I stayed with them every single time," Aikin said. She added that she was "very close to Stacy," having been present both at her birth and the birth of her sister, Cassandra.

Aikin found Drew Peterson to be pleasant company, but she was reluctant to stay with the couple and their children if the family was embroiled in domestic strife. While Stacy told Aikin she was going to end the marriage, she assured her aunt that her presence in the home would not be a problem. Aikin did end up staying with them.

"They were getting ready for a divorce, she said, before I came," Aikin recalled. "She said it wouldn't be uncomfortable, but it was different than the other times I was out there."

Aikin wasn't the only person with whom Stacy shared her plan to leave Peterson. Sharon Bychowski attested that Stacy also talked about wanting to leave, as did Scott Rossetto, with whom Stacy exchanged racy text messages in the months before her disappearance and who later testified before the grand jury investigating the case. Pamela Bosco, Cassandra's legal guardian and family spokeswoman, also said Stacy wanted to take her children and get away from Peterson. She said Stacy had asked Cassandra about moving in with Bosco's brothers in California.

But there was other information, more shocking than her intention to end her marriage, that Stacy supposedly played close to the vest in the months before October 28, reportedly confiding in only two men.

One of those men was a Wheaton, Illinois attorney named Harry Smith, whom Stacy contacted to discuss divorcing her husband. Smith represented Savio in her divorce from Peterson.

The other man was minister Neil Schori, formerly of Westbrook Christian Church, a nondenominational congregation where Stacy and Drew Peterson sometimes attended services. On December 10, the minister told his story to Greta Van Susteren on her cable news show. After the show aired, Schori, a tall, congenial man, was reluctant to tell his tale again or be perceived as trying to capitalize on Stacy's misfortune. At the same time, he told me that he does not want Stacy to be forgotten or for her case to fade away before justice can be done, and that he stood by all the statements he made on that broadcast.

On the show, Schori said Stacy telephoned him in August of 2007. Stacy had not been to church in a few months, and Schori had not seen her during that time. Her call came at the cusp of a hectic and eventful time for Schori's own family. His wife, Brandi, gave birth to twin daughters in early October. Then, in November, he left Westbrook Christian Church to be installed as lead pastor at Naperville Christian Church. But in August, those events were still ahead of him; he agreed to see Stacy.

The pair met the next day in a Bolingbrook coffee shop. Stacy filled him in on the troubles in her marriage, but Schori sensed there was something more she wanted to tell him.

"Well, I try not to push people into an area that they're not comfortable, and I gave her—I gave her an out," said Schori, who has a master's degree from Lincoln Christian College and participated in two counseling-related internships.

"I said, 'If you'd like to share it with me, I'm here to hear it.' I said, 'But there's no pressure. You don't have to feel like you have to share anything you're not comfortable with.'"

What Stacy told him, Schori said, was, "He did it."

Schori said he believed he knew what Stacy was talking about, but "needed clarification." They had never before broached the subject of wife number three.

"I had just heard casual conversations in the community and in my own church about speculation over an interesting death of Mr. Peterson's wife, his third wife," he told Van Susteren.

When Schori pressed Stacy to explain what she was talking about, he recalled, she said, "He killed Kathleen."

"And I was really blown away," Schori said. "I was reeling inside."

"I asked for more specific things. She gave me details that I really can't share. But I just got her talking about it and asked her what—this is a crazy amount of information. Again, I asked her, 'What exactly can I do with this? Why did you tell me?' I asked her if she had ever told anyone else. She said, at the time, she had never told another person."

Schori said Stacy provided him with "specific information about [Peterson] not being in the house" the night of Kathleen Savio's death. Stacy told Schori that she discussed Peterson's absence with him "shortly after" the evening in question, and that she knew what had transpired at her husband's old house on Pheasant Chase Drive.

"It was more than just putting two and two together," he said. "It was not speculation on her part." What it was, he confirmed, was a confession by Peterson to his new young wife.

Police had interviewed Stacy about Savio's death, but she did not tell them the story she told Schori, the minister said.

"I believe she was simply afraid," he said, noting that even three years later, he did not believe she intended to tell police.

When Schori got back to Westbrook Christian Church after his disquieting conversation with Stacy, something perhaps even more unsettling awaited him: a voice mail message from Drew Peterson. He wanted to meet with the minister.

Schori called Peterson back. "He just said, 'Hey, I'm just trying to get a hold of you. I thought maybe we could meet since you just met with Stacy.' And I—I sort of backed out of doing that," Schori said.

"Your heart must have been in your shoes when you got that voice mail," said Van Susteren.

"Oh, my gosh," Schori said. "Sure."

Peterson's attorney, Joel Brodsky, went on the offensive the very next night. In an interview with Dan Abrams on MSNBC, Brodsky said that he'd heard rumors of a romantic connection between Stacy and the minister.

The attorney explained he had received "several calls" on the subject but added, "I don't know if there is any validity to it."

An incredulous Abrams asked Brodsky, "You guys are going to slime a man of the cloth now on this one?"

"Believe me, that's not something I started," Brodsky replied. "People call me."

Brodsky later admitted the "rumors" he had heard were spoken by Peterson himself. The "people" who'd called him must have been Peterson.

Schori denied any involvement or romantic entanglement with Stacy and warned Brodsky to back off. Peterson said he could not comment on Schori's feelings for his wife, but said he had no doubt Stacy had the hots for the minister.

"All I know for sure is, Stacy had a big crush on him," Peterson told me. "Every time she went to see him, she was all dolled up, all sexied up."

Brodsky went a step further and said he was told Stacy would put on a bikini top and roar by Westbrook Christian Church on her motorcycle to catch the minister's attention. Again, the man that he said had informed him of this was none other than Peterson.

Stacy and Schori may never have had anything more than a tense conversation in a coffee shop, but early on in the investigation into her disappearance, a man from her past surfaced. It turned out that he had been trading lascivious text messages and carrying on flirty phone conversations with Stacy in the weeks leading up to October 28. The man—thirty-five-year-old male nurse Scott Rossetto—said that the text message and phone sessions were the extent of their relationship, which stopped short of anything physical. Based on the content and specificity of the text messages, however, police thought the relationship went much further. The text messages have never been released to the public.

Rossetto and his twin brother, Keith Rossetto, also a male nurse, testified before a special grand jury investigating Stacy's disappearance and Savio's death. The grand jury convened in November of 2007 for a six-month term with the option to extend for another four months; all proceedings of the grand jury are closed.

Keith Rossetto had spent time with Stacy in the months before he left for the Army and she met Peterson, though Keith denies that they actually dated. While both knew Stacy when she was a single girl, it was Scott who interacted with her in the weeks before she vanished.

On November 21, 2007, with Stacy missing for nearly a month, the Rossetto brothers testified before the grand jury. The goateed identical twins were dressed in almost-matching clothing, topped with dark stocking caps pulled low on their shaved heads.

"They were like something out of a Coen brothers movie," observed one official.

When they were younger, the Rossetto brothers dreamt of fame, and not the kind that comes from testifying about a woman whom police believe may have been killed by her husband, a woman with whom the police suspect one or both of the twins may have slept. The brothers had been a singing duet since they performed "Jesus Loves Me" together at a church when they were two years old, and in the mid-1990s they had aspirations to make it in Nashville. Those aspirations had evaporated by November 2007.

"So much for that," Keith said to me when I brought up their erstwhile musical dreams. After making his appearance before the grand jury, Keith was on his way home; his twin brother remained upstairs answering questions.

A few days before he went in front of the grand jury, Scott Rossetto told *The Herald News* that he had not heard from Stacy in about six years when "all of a sudden she called me out of the blue about three weeks before she disappeared." She told him that "she was just going through some stuff and just found my phone number," and divulged the troubles in her marriage and her thoughts about leaving her husband.

For the next week or two, Scott and Stacy kept in touch, he said. They flirted on the phone and sent each other racy text messages for maybe twelve days. A few months later he was explaining himself to a grand jury.

The line of questioning was not accusatory, he said, although a prosecutor asked him if he "did anything" to Stacy. The most he did to her was send her "perverted and flirty" text messages, he said, and met with her one time, nine days before she vanished, at a Bolingbrook Denny's restaurant.

Drew Peterson showed up too. Stacy had let him know about her plans, Rossetto said. She and Drew had argued about her going to meet with Scott, but she went anyway. So her husband, in uniform and in his squad car, made a point of checking up on his wife that night.

Rossetto said the uniformed Peterson stared at Stacy but did not raise his voice, exhibit anger or make any threats.

"He asked me how I'd feel if my wife went off with another guy," Scott said. "[He] just kept staring at her. He sat with us for about a good fifteen, twenty minutes."

Even before this uncomfortable encounter with Peterson, whom he knew of from his brother's past liaison with Stacy, Scott said he was not tempted to dive into an adulterous affair.

"She was a married woman," he said. "She was married to a Bolingbrook police officer. I didn't need that kind of misery."

If the police were correct in their speculation, Peterson may have been trying very hard, with the help of his stepbrother, Tom Morphey, to ensure that Scott Rossetto received well more than his share of misery. In the early days of Stacy's disappearance, before the twins' grand jury appearance, state police conducted searches around Scott Rossetto's home in the Village of Shorewood, a burgeoning but still relatively small bedroom community about fifteen miles from Peterson's cul-de-sac. The searches did not register with the public as particularly important at the time, but within weeks, the state police's reasons for poking around out there became quite clear.

The week before the Rossetto twins went before the grand jury, a pair of law enforcement sources divulged why the police were searching Scott Rossetto's town: not because Rossetto was a suspect—he wasn't—but because, as one of the sources said, "If you knew your wife had a boyfriend, you'd put the body by him."

Another police source on the Peterson case told me investigators speculated that the night Stacy vanished, her husband took her cell phone with him to Shorewood and dialed his own phone. He had left his telephone back in Bolingbrook, the source said, and when the call went through, it would show that Stacy's phone was somewhere near Scott Rossetto's residence and that his own was in Bolingbrook, where it belonged. That way, the call would "ping" off cell towers in Shorewood, leading investigators to believe Stacy had made the call herself while she was with Rossetto. According to a column by Michael Sneed of the *Chicago Sun-Times*, Peterson had some help with this plan. The day after Sheryl Alcox said her boyfriend, Tom Morphey, was away at "therapy," Sneed broke a story painting Peterson's unemployed stepbrother not as a bumbling patsy but as an active accomplice who helped "dispose" of a troublesome wife.

Sneed extensively quoted a solid "source close to the investigation" who pegged self-preservation as Peterson's motive. Stacy posed a threat to him: Her existence jeopardized not only his financial security, but his freedom.

"Sneed hears Stacy Peterson told a clergyman in August that her husband had claimed to have killed his former wife, Kathleen Savio, and made it look like an accident," Sneed said in a November 29 column, apparently referring to Schori.

Not only that, the source said, but "the day Stacy disappeared, she told Peterson she was leaving him and issued this ultimatum: She was going to begin divorce proceedings and she wanted him out of the house by Wednesday...."

Sneed's column continued: "The source believes it was the day of Stacy's ultimatum that her life may have ended. Stacy had told friends recently that if she disappeared, it wouldn't be her doing."

And that, according to Sneed's source, was where Morphey came in.

Sneed's source provided a timeline for the late afternoon and evening of the last day Stacy was seen alive. It picked up about six hours or so after Stacy supposedly left her home and family, and three and a half hours before her "Dear Drew" call to Peterson.

By 5 p.m., according to Sneed's source, Peterson called in to take the day off work. At 7 p.m., he met Morphey at a local Starbucks and discussed "the problems he was having with Stacy and how to dispose of the problem."

"Peterson reportedly excused himself and left Morphey in the coffee shop with Peterson's cell phone, which he told Morphey *not* to answer if it rang," Sneed wrote. "The phone did ring after Peterson's departure and the name 'Stacy' appeared on the caller ID."

Sneed went on to say, "Later that evening, Morphey was again summoned by Peterson—only this time to his home, where he reportedly asked Morphey for help removing a blue plastic barrel, which Morphey later described to police as feeling warm, and loaded it into a sports utility vehicle, sources said."

Morphey reportedly attempted suicide the next day by overdosing on liquor and pills. He was taken to Edward Hospital in Naperville for treatment. Peterson openly admits he stopped by the hospital to pay his stepbrother a visit. The two must have had quite a lot of catching up to do.

Another pinging of Peterson's cell phone the night of October 28 led state police to coordinate underwater searches of stretches of the Chicago Sanitary and Ship Canal in and around the nearby towns of Lockport and Romeoville, a police source told me.

Stacy's sister Cassandra Cales claims to have called Peterson's cell phone about 11 o'clock that night from the nearby Meijer department store parking lot. Stacy was last seen that morning.

Cales said Peterson sounded out of breath and told her he was at his home. But Cales said that she had been outside of his house shortly before she made the call, and he was nowhere to be found.

The police source said cell phone records showed Peterson was somewhere near Romeoville by the Sanitary and Ship Canal.

"When Cassandra called Drew's phone, it pinged near that area," the source said.

In response, divers searched the canal floor, using high-tech equipment and watercraft, which required the clearing of abandoned, submerged automobiles. The searches turned up nothing.

Despite the lead that put police there, my source called one of the searches a "complete waste of time" and was not impressed with the operation as a whole. Even with the high-tech underwater cameras, the searches were leaning on luck and battling long odds. Apparently, locating a body in the Sanitary and Ship Canal, which runs twenty-four feet deep and over two hundred feet wide, is akin to finding the proverbial needle in a haystack. Visibility in the canal was limited to about half a foot, the source told me, and for the camera to catch a peek of Stacy or a blue barrel, it would "have to bump into it."

"I think they're just trying to show they looked, she's not in there, and move on to the next location. If they do [find the blue barrel supposedly containing Stacy's remains]," the source said before the searches were called off, "it's because God wants them to, because there's no way they're going to find it in that muck."

Peterson has his own version of events of October 28, the day he last saw his wife. When he recounted it to me, while sitting behind a desk in his house on Halloween night, he didn't mention Tom Morphey once.

The last time he laid eyes on his wife, Peterson said, was midmorning on October 28, a Sunday. He admitted to having skipped out of work early, returning home about three or four a.m. Peterson said he hit the hay at that time but woke up at about 9 o'clock to the din of his children jumping around. He said he "believes" Stacy was still in the house, but he could not be sure because, having just woken up, he did not fully trust his memory.

Peterson does remember his wife telling him she was leaving to help Bruce Zidarich, a friend of her sister, paint the former home of her brother, Yelton Cales, in Yorkville, which was a good half hour away.

At the time of Stacy's disappearance, Yelton Cales was back in prison at Western Illinois Correctional Center for violating his parole. Peterson said the family had leased the Yorkville home for him to serve out a house-arrest sentence. He couldn't stay with his father, Anthony, Peterson said, because he lived too close to a school to house a registered sex offender. Peterson said his wife, who favored bright and vibrant colors, painted the rented house in bold hues for her brother. Stacy's next-door neighbor Bychowski added that Stacy even gave the decor an Asian flair to make her brother "happy" during his house arrest.

"She painted the wall red on one side. She did a theme like a Chinese theme," Bychowski said. "She bought him a bedspread with her [own] money so he could have a Chinese bedroom, because he loves Chinese." Bychowski said Stacy also arranged for her brother's ride home from prison and installed a telephone in the house.

Yelton, however, did not get to enjoy his Chinese decor for long before being dragged back to prison, so on that Sunday, Stacy and Zidarich were going to repaint the house and break the lease. Peterson said he thinks his wife left about eleven in the morning, but once again he said he could not be sure.

Zidarich reportedly last spoke to Stacy about 10:15 that morning. Stacy never showed up to paint. Her sister Cassandra had spent the day waiting to hear from her. Cassandra allegedly said Stacy didn't pick up her cell phone when she called that afternoon, or any of the other times she tried ringing her that day.

The next time Peterson said he heard from his wife was about 9 p.m., when she called his cell phone. He said she wanted to let him know she had met another man and abandoned her family. That's the story he's stuck with ever since: Stacy ran off with another man.

Bychowski too has her own timeline of that day, and through sheer repetition—to the cops, grand jury, and numerous reporters—even the most minute details appear burned into her brain and capable of being summoned automatically.

That Sunday, she called the Peterson house at "five to twelve," she said. Kristopher answered, and when she asked to speak to his mom, Bychowski said he sounded a little disoriented, responding, "Um, uh, uh, hold on."

"Drew picked up the phone," Bychowski continued, "and said, 'Hey Shar-on'—that's what Lacy called me, Shar-on—'what's up?' And I said, 'Where's Stace?' 'Oh, she went to her grandpa's to run some errands.'"

Bychowski believes Peterson did not know then of his wife's plans to accompany Zidarich to Yorkville.

"It's odd, isn't it? Yes," Bychowski said. "He didn't know. I don't believe he knew that she had already talked to Bruce about cleaning the house. So there's a difference of story right here, right from the get-go."

But at the time Sharon called, she had an entirely mundane purpose: to give the kids some lollipops she'd bought for them. So Peterson brought Kristopher, Anthony, and Lacy over after they'd eaten lunch, around 1 p.m. He asked her to watch the three children while he took care of some business.

"By the time he got actually in the car, it was about 1:15," Bychowski said. "And then he came right back at 1:30, because I was still outside. Then I went inside about 1:30 to do the rest of my work. Then I started wrapping Christmas presents."

About a half hour later, around 2 p.m., Bychowski called Stacy's cell phone. The call went straight to voice mail, which struck Bychowski as odd. "When she's gone, she never turned her cell off, ever."

Bychowski did not hear from Stacy for the rest of the day. At about 8:30 a.m. the next morning—Monday, October 29—her doorbell rang. She expected it to be Stacy, who usually rang the bell and walked right in. This time, though, it was Peterson. He grabbed Bychowski by the arm and, saying he needed her, took her to his house. She didn't even have time to put on her shoes.

"I thought, 'Oh, my God. Oh, my God, what's wrong?' My heart is pounding, that kind of pounding when you get pulled over by the cops?... [I asked,] 'What's wrong? What's wrong?' [Drew said,] 'Just come, come.' He wouldn't tell me, I see that there's both cars in the driveway."

Once she was inside Peterson's house, he dropped what he must have thought was a bombshell, only Bychowski knew it was coming.

"He says, 'She left me,'" Bychowski said. "I go, 'Yeah'.... I'm thinking, 'And?' 'Cause I know how unhappy she is, and I know she wants to leave him. I thought she left for sure.

"I said, 'Where are the kids?' And he says, 'They're upstairs.'"

With this revelation, she knew something was amiss.

"He goes, 'I know this is really difficult for you. I know you thought she was your bud and all.' I'm like, 'Now what do I do?' I'm in the house alone with him, basically. And you know what else was odd? Everything was perfect. Like, we have the same flowers. They're always on her kitchen table. Gone. There's nothing on the kitchen table. No kids' place mats. No sippy cups. Nothing. Odd."

Peterson then complained of Stacy looting their safe and going on a spending spree. He said she took $25,000 from their safe at home, Bychowski said, but Stacy had told Bychowski the week before that she had transferred $25,000 to pay off a home-equity line of credit so they would only have to divide up assets and not liabilities. "But he doesn't know that I know that," Bychowski said. "So I just said, 'Oh.'"

Peterson said Stacy also took passports and car and house titles, and bought herself new clothes and a bikini. The list gave Bychowski further cause for concern.

"Well, I also know that she has a favorite bikini. She's not going to give that up. I know she has these fabulous bras that she bought herself as a treat after she had her liposuction. I said, 'She's not giving up those bras.' I know her. She had favorite bras. She's not giving up all those bras."

Bychowski was in disbelief. She figured Stacy would leave Peterson sooner or later, but she could not swallow that the young woman would abruptly depart without taking her children. When she got home and briefed her husband, she said he had a similar sense of dread.

"I said, 'Bob, the kids are there.' He sits up and he goes, 'Okay, that's not right.' I said, 'You don't think I'm being a drama queen to tell you that I think that there's something wrong with this?' And he goes, 'One thing I know about her is, she'd never leave her kids.'

"My husband's not involved with a lot of stuff," Bychowski said, "but he knows her well enough to know those kids are always with her."

Soon after Bychowski returned home, Stacy's sister Cassandra and Bruce Zidarich were at her door.

Zidarich asked Bychowski if she'd heard about Stacy; Bychowski said she had. Stacy's sister, Bychowski said, was crying.

Cassandra had apparently had a sleepless, stressful night. After not hearing from Stacy all day Sunday, around eleven that evening she had gone to her sister's house. The driveway was empty. She said she spoke with her nephew Kristopher who told her his parents had fought that morning, then Stacy had left, and his father was out looking for her.

Cassandra left the house and called Peterson on his cell phone. She was sitting in the parking lot of a nearby Meijer department store when he told her that Stacy had run off, and he was trying to find her. She said Peterson also told her he was home, which she found difficult to believe, considering she had just been there.

Cassandra then went to the Downers Grove Police Department. She did not want to trust the matter to the Bolingbrook police, and might have chosen the Downers Grove police because she had grown up in the town, but they sent her to Bolingbrook anyway.

From the Bolingbrook Police Department, Cassandra drove by her sister's home again. This time, both the Denali and the Grand Prix were parked there. Cassandra then headed to the nearby District 5 state police headquarters and, in the early hours of Monday, October 29, reported Stacy Peterson missing.

By the time Cassandra showed up at Bychowski's house, she had an awful feeling about what had happened to her sister.

"She said, 'He killed her. He killed her,'" Bychowski said.

"One thing I know about Stacy is she would never leave with anybody without calling Cassandra," Bychowski continued. "She would never let her sister cry on TV. She absolutely, unconditionally loves Cassandra—no matter what. No matter how stupid Cassandra acts. She totally loves Cassandra."

Monday ended and Tuesday morning came with no sign of Stacy on Pheasant Chase Court. It was the third day Bychowski would not hear from her friend, but the missing woman's husband kept coming over and calling. At around 9 a.m., he rang his neighbor's phone to give her his predictions for the day ahead.

"He goes, 'This is what's going to happen today. The media, the media will be coming today.'"

Bychowski remembered her surprise and confusion, and asked Peterson what he was talking about.

She said Peterson told her, "Well, because you know Bruce thinks I hurt Stacy. You know, Bruce and Cassandra think I hurt her. So now the media's going to be coming today."

She said Peterson wanted her to move one of his cars into her driveway so reporters would not know he was home. He called her again when he was out at the airport with his kids, putting a sticker on his plane. The media was coming, he said, and he didn't want them to know if he was there or not.

Bychowski said her secretary talked her out of doing him the favor—"Sharon, do not get in that car. Are you out of your mind?"—so Bychowski told Peterson that she didn't think it was a good idea.

"He said, 'Can you just wear gloves?'" Apparently he assumed that her concern was about leaving fingerprints. Bychowski coolly responded, "Uh, no. I don't think that's a good idea either."

In the end he just put his car in her driveway himself, Bychowski said. On Wednesday, he informed her that he "may or may not need" to move his car back over to her house again, she said, but called back to tell her about a change in plans: His stepbrother, it seemed, tried to commit suicide, and Peterson was going to visit him in the hospital.

Upon his return, Bychowski asked how his stepbrother was making out, and Peterson sounded puzzled.

"He goes, 'What? Oh, well, he lost his job, lost his family—go figure,'" Bychowski said. "I thought, 'Ooh, you guys must not be too close to him.' Just kind of the way he said it was very flippant."

Peterson wasn't the only one asking favors. Also on Tuesday, Bychowski said, a state police sergeant called and asked her if she could babysit the children next door, because the state police were taking Peterson in for questioning. Instead, they ended up talking to him at home for about an hour and a half, Bychowski said, so Peterson was still around at 5:30 in the afternoon when he rang her doorbell again and asked if she could take Anthony to an evening daycare program.

That Wednesday was Halloween, and Bychowski, determined that the children not miss their holiday fun, took them trick-or-treating.

"About 4 o'clock [Peterson] called me and we passed the kids over the back fence with their outfits. And then I brought them in here and changed them into Superman and Tinkerbell." To avoid the media, Bychowski drove the kids—minus Kristopher, who went on his own—down the street.

"If you get out of the car two blocks away, no one will know who you are," Bychowski observed, and reported that the children enjoyed themselves despite the unsettling circumstances surrounding the day.

The day after Halloween, a Thursday, was not nearly as much fun. The state police took Peterson in for questioning, and then they served a search warrant on his home. Needless to say, the children were upset. Bychowski said a neighbor told her the cops were grabbing Stacy's kids.

"One had Lacy in his arms," she said. The little girl was screaming, "like bloodcurdling screaming outside," so Bychowski took her into her house and soothed her.

Later in the day, Bychowski said she had Peterson, his children, a pair of police officers, television personality Greta Van Susteren and her crew, Cassandra Cales and her friend Bruce, and Kathleen Savio's sister Anna Marie Doman all packed into her house while the cops searched Peterson's home and property. Bychowski said Peterson told her they needed to talk and led her into her tiny powder room.

"He walks in with me and he says, 'Well, it's been a long time since I've had a chick in the bathroom.' And I'm like, 'Okay, and we are in here because...?' He goes, 'Okay, should they arrest me, I want to make sure my kids go to Steve [Stephen, Peterson's grown son from his first marriage]. You've got his number. Call him right away, and he'll come and get the kids.'"

Bychowski said he expected the police to take him in for seventy-two hours. "'A seventy-two-hour hold,' he said. 'We do it all the time.'"

The Bolingbrook police might have done it all the time, but the state police did not pull that on Peterson. They did not run him in, and when they were done rummaging through his house and seizing his cars and various other possessions, he returned home with his children.

Friday brought another call from Peterson, Bychowski said—again, to ask a favor. He wanted to move the kids through her house to send them off with Stephen and avoid the media massing in front of his house. Drew, Stephen, and the kids arrived with some packed clothes at her back door. Bychowski was surprised to see Kristopher there in the middle of a school day. She said the boy told her his father said he could stay home; his brother, Thomas, however, was at school.

"Odd," Bychowski said. "So I said to Drew, 'How come Tom went to school but Kris didn't?' He said, 'Well, I thought he could help out with the little kids.' I don't believe that. I think Kris knew too much, and he wanted to get him out of there. Kris is the one that stuttered when I said, 'Where's your mom?' Kris is the one who heard them fighting in the morning and told Cassandra, and Kris is the one he takes out of school on Friday."

Bychowski said she sent Stephen Peterson back for the children's winter coats, boots and gloves. Lacy did not want to leave but was finally taken away. That was the last Bychowski saw of Drew Peterson until he returned home the following Thursday. That night, Bychowski claims, Peterson peered in her windows and was "yelling" at her. Peterson maintains he was merely attempting to pass off the ashes of Stacy's deceased half sister, Tina.

Two days after this incident, Geraldo Rivera landed in Bolingbrook and commandeered Bychowski's house, lining up just about every player involved in the drama and stashing them inside her home.

Without a doubt, life on Pheasant Chase Court had taken a surreal turn.

"It's just, I mean, look at how bizarre this is," Bychowski said.

It was bizarre. And the strange days were just beginning.

CHAPTER NINE

Drew Peterson acted like a hunted man when the media first came calling to ask questions about his last two wives: both the one reported missing the final Monday morning of October 2007, and the other found dead in her bathtub a few years before. Peterson opened his front door just wide enough for one eyeball to peer out. The glass in and around the door was plastered with sheets of white paper, and the blinds were kept drawn over the large front windows. When he cracked open his door and looked out with one eye, he was terse and appeared nervous. It wouldn't take long for him to emerge from his shell.

Though he initially was reluctant to appear on camera or leave his house after Stacy was gone, soon Peterson was inviting reporters into his home for interviews. Then, in short order, Peterson was venturing outside to banter with the camera crews, reporters and photographers keeping constant vigil in his cul-de-sac, waiting for something to happen—either for Peterson to pull some outrageous stunt or for the police to swoop in and snatch him up. And while an O.J. Simpson-style slow-speed car chase along Interstate 55 might have been asking for too much, Peterson's behavior was so odd that it couldn't be ruled out. Unfortunately for the media swarm outside 6 Pheasant Chase Court, the police did disappointingly little swooping or snatching, although Peterson fulfilled his part by clowning around for the cameras and mouthing no shortage of memorable quotes.

As the days went by without the law making a move, Peterson grew bolder. At one point in the initial days of his wife's disappearance, he chatted with former Los Angeles homicide detective turned television personality Mark Fuhrman, famous for his star turn in the O.J. case and later for writing a book about the decades-old Martha Moxley murder that led to the trial and conviction of Kennedy relative Michael Skakel.

Then, about two weeks after Stacy Peterson vanished, Geraldo Rivera rode into town. The man who stared Charles Manson in the eye, who reported from war zones and uncovered the broken bottles hidden away in Al Capone's vault, had touched down in Bolingbrook, and he wanted to talk to Drew Peterson.

Rivera actually did accomplish this. He ventured inside Peterson's home and spoke with him off camera. When he emerged, Rivera reported to his audience that there was a tightening noose around the neck of Peterson, who remained inside his home, hiding from the television cameras while Rivera broadcast from a perch in front of the house.

Peterson later told me his conversation with Rivera was relaxed and cordial. He said he watched the live broadcast with family and friends as soon as Rivera left his house and was both shocked and amused by the television personality depicting him as a frightened man with a noose around his neck.

"Geraldo Rivera, the nuisance of news," Peterson called him.

Geraldo would go on to dub Peterson the "skunk of Bolingbrook." In turn, Peterson appeared on the *Today* show and told host Matt Lauer that his only regret in the months following Stacy's disappearance was "letting Geraldo Rivera in my house. Nothing other than that."

After his chat with Peterson, Geraldo camped out next door at the home of Sharon and Bob Bychowski, where quite a crowd was assembled. Besides Geraldo and his assorted staff were neighbors of Lisa Stebic, a missing woman from nearby Plainfield, who vanished about six months before Stacy and whose story was rapidly losing public interest as a result of the drama on Pheasant Chase; Melissa and Charlie Doman, the niece and nephew of Kathleen Savio; Steve Carcerano, Kathleen and Drew's neighbor from their time down the street as man and wife; and Debbie Forgue, the half sister of Stacy's deceased half sister, Tina Ryan. At one point Debbie's husband, Martin Forgue, went over to Peterson's home to retrieve Ryan's ashes. Meanwhile, Rivera tried, and failed, to get people inside the house to proclaim that a hostage situation over the ashes was unfolding next door.

"It was absolutely crazy," Sharon Bychowski said. "This is the biggest thing in our whole life we'll ever be through. I mean, think about it. Could there be anything bigger than somebody murdering their wife next door to your house? I don't think so." (Despite what his next-door neighbor may think, Peterson still has not been charged— at least as of the beginning of summer 2008—with murder or any other offense related to the death of his third wife or the disappearance of his fourth.)

Bychowski said Geraldo's staff members had wormed their way inside her house earlier in the day. They began by asking if they could do a feed from the backyard; then they wanted to move onto the patio. Bychowski agreed. Afterwards, they asked if Geraldo could actually sit at her kitchen table but leave the booms and equipment outside. Again, she agreed.

"But now the booms are inside," Bychowski said. "So it gets crazier and crazier. Finally they say, 'We're just going to do it, we're just going to stand up.'" They took down a $300 lamp, to protect it from being hit by a boom. "And they moved my kitchen table. Now all the cameras are here, then he moved my husband's chair. You're kind of in the middle of it, what are you going to do? You're going to say no? He said, 'I promise you, no matter what, we are going to put every single thing back where we found it. You will be absolutely one hundred percent happy when we leave.' And we were. They were very nice. They called me the next day: 'Did we put back everything we moved in your house? Is there anything we didn't do? Is there anyone I can call for you? Cleaning? Did you check out everything?'"

Everything, Bychowski said, checked out just fine.

Bychowski had spent the previous night in a La Quinta hotel to get away from all the media lunacy on the street—and from Peterson, who she says was shouting at her over their fence and standing at her window the night before that. When she returned to her home, the scene outside it had only grown more surreal.

"Out in front are all the Stebic people," she said. "They all come in. They're all on my couch. It was nuts. Charlie and Melissa [Doman] were here. It was crazy. It wasn't supposed to be in my house. [Rivera] wanted to use my backyard. It wasn't that cold. He just had his jacket on. Charlie, Melissa, Stebic people, [Steve] Carcerano.... It was absolutely crazy."

Not all the action was in Bychowski's house, or even on Pheasant Chase Court. Geraldo had conducted an earlier interview in the back seat of a car in an "undisclosed location" with Ric Mims, who only days before had been Peterson's staunchest supporter. Mims, who had steadfastly defended Drew and proclaimed his close friend's innocence, apparently had an abrupt change of heart. He also seemed to be very afraid, hence his backseat interview in the undisclosed location.

Meanwhile, at Bychowski's house, Geraldo moved from subject to subject, and at one point appeared to instigate a confrontation between Savio's nephew, Charlie Doman, and Carcerano, the man who would eventually take Mims' place as Peterson's chief flunky.

The role of Drew's friend and defender provided Carcerano with some notoriety, but it was not all cable television interviews and curious gazes while he was out on the town with Peterson. In fact, Carcerano told me of a nasty confrontation with a disapproving woman who recognized him as supporter of Peterson when he was just trying to get some color at a local tanning salon. But in the same conversation he also mentioned to me that—if he could not appear as himself—he hoped former 'N Sync boy-bander Joey Fatone (whom he believes resembles him) would play his part when a movie is made of Drew Peterson's story.

But before there was a movie, there was Geraldo, and Carcerano told the Fox News Network personality how he was there the night Savio's body was found in her bathtub. Doman did not believe this, and later told me he had never heard of Carcerano before the Geraldo taping. He had always been under the impression that another neighbor and friend of his aunt had been the only one to go into the house and make the grisly discovery while Peterson waited outside.

Visibly angry, Doman seemed on the verge of attacking Carcerano before Geraldo stepped between them. When I spoke with Carcerano about this incident, he told me he was not scared. If Doman had attacked him, he told me, it would have been a big mistake. But that wasn't what came across on television.

While Bychowski willingly opened her home to Geraldo from the beginning and has given numerous interviews in the months since Stacy disappeared, another neighbor was not as welcoming to the army of media; apparently, he considered the state of his lawn to be of a significantly higher priority. This homeowner strung yellow police tape around his front yard to keep the press from trampling over it. Peterson himself at one point posted no-trespassing signs and placed orange traffic cones at the edge of his driveway, but they did little to keep the media away. Warning signs and traffic cones aside, Peterson did not particularly seem to *want* the media to stay away.

Peterson displayed his zeal for appearing on television—or, at the very least, seeing his name in print—within days of Stacy's disappearance. By Halloween, he had started entertaining reporters inside his home. The same night, Greta Van Susteren—who drove this story in the media as she did the Natalee Holloway missing-person's case less than three years earlier—broadcast live across the street from his home for the first time.

On Halloween, Peterson granted me an audience as he sat behind his desk, the one topped by boxes disguised as classic books like *A Tale of Two Cities* and *War and Peace*. He took questions and was gracious and expansive with his answers. As I listened, the inherently creepy Ric Mims lurked in the background. At the time, Mims was Peterson's staunchest supporter, whose responsibilities involved answering the door for Peterson and running interference for him. In fact, when I got inside and noticed Mims lingering mere inches from Peterson, I asked, "Who are you?"

"I'm his brother," Mims said.

"No, he's not," Peterson said from behind his desk, not bothering to glance at the longtime friend who was about to betray him in his greatest time of need.

Mims continued to skulk around throughout my conversation with Peterson. He also answered the door when trick-or-treaters rang.

Peterson's children, back from their own trick-or-treating, also milled about. It was disturbing to have a four-year-old playing at my feet while his father detailed the death of his third wife and the supposed adulterous affair that prompted his fourth wife, the four-year-old's mother, to abandon the family.

"I believe, like I tell everyone, she's not missing," Peterson told me that night. "She's gone on her own. And it's not by nothing that I did."

This could not have been an easy thing for a man like Peterson to admit. Granted, closing in on fifty-four he was no longer young, and it must have been tough to keep up with a woman who had thirty years less mileage, a woman who had blossomed from the seventeen-year-old kid he'd first met into a twenty-three-year-old with bigger breasts, surgically sculpted legs, and a new flatter stomach. Still, he was Drew Peterson, former undercover narcotics officer, then sergeant in charge of the overnight shift, when the streets of Bolingbrook are at their most desolate. And he was a Lothario, married four times and, by his own admission, unfaithful to the first three wives. As Mims put it in an interview on CNN, "He was a big flirt with the ladies," and a lot of people in town knew it.

"I wouldn't say a womanizer," Mims added, "but just overly flirtatious, chasing a little bit here and there."

Still, Drew was man enough to admit it when the tables were turned and he was the cuckold, left home alone with the kids while his young wife was off gallivanting only God knew where. And that was just what he did on Halloween night, suggesting that the rabbit gene might run in the family, since Stacy's mother had run off herself about eight years before.

The day after Halloween, things became even more curious. The cliché "media horde" could have been defined by an aerial photograph of Peterson's cul-de-sac. And the legion only grew once the state police showed up to execute a search warrant.

The cops seized both Peterson's GMC Denali and the Pontiac Grand Prix he had purchased for Stacy. They grabbed computers, compact discs, iPods and his collection of eleven guns. Cadaver dogs and their handlers poked around Peterson's property and home. Rumors—repeated to this day despite a lack of evidence to confirm them—swirled in the packed cul-de-sac that the dogs had hit on something in the master bedroom, although that was never found to be true.

For much of this spectacle, Peterson was sequestered next door at the Bychowski's. Perhaps as a cop-to-former-cop courtesy, he allowed Fuhrman in to speak with him, but managed to stay out of view, at least until he could no longer resist stepping—or catapulting himself—into the media spotlight.

Peterson accomplished this by ambling out the Bychowskis' back door in the late afternoon and down their driveway. He made sure he attracted attention by masking himself with an American flag bandanna and dark sunglasses, and pulling an NYPD baseball cap low over his eyes.

He stood there in the driveway until a few reporters noticed him and walked over to ask questions. He accepted a compliment for his bandanna but had time for little else. When the camera crews finally caught sight of him and rushed over, Peterson said, "Oh, I got to run away," and did just that.

Mims, who on November 1 was still in Peterson's corner, denied that the man behind the mask was his pal Peterson. Few, if any, took Mims seriously, which was a running theme throughout the saga of Stacy's disappearance. And Mims soon showed himself to be a pretty lousy friend, much less a brother. Once the embattled cop's most vocal ally, Mims turned on Peterson and sold a story to the *National Enquirer* which included the line, "Mims says [Drew's son Kristopher] had heard his parents fighting, an argument that police and Mims believe ended in murder."

Mims would not say how much he was paid for the story. When asked about the friend who betrayed him, Peterson said, "Our hero. He was out to make some money, and he got his thirty seconds of fame, so God love him."

The sight of Peterson standing in his next-door neighbor's driveway, resplendent in his red, white and blue bandanna, NYPD cap and glasses, became an enduring visual in the case. Other images also became instantly memorable: Peterson, again in his bandanna mask, on his motorcycle, roaring down his driveway past the press, and earning the *Chicago Sun-Times* headline "Easy Rider"; Peterson, armed with a handheld video camera, filming the camera crews outside his home while they filmed him; the broadcast of Peterson on the *Today* show, blaming his marital problems with the wife nobody could find on "her menstrual cycle."

"I'm not trying to be funny here," Peterson said to preface his remarks, all the while clearly trying to be funny, "but Stacy would ask me for a divorce after her sister died on a regular basis. I'm not trying to be funny. And it was based on her menstrual cycle."

One thing Peterson was consistent about was his effort to be funny. And as he grew increasingly glib, one attorney told me that if the embattled ex-cop had retained him, he would have "fired him" as a client if he did not agree to shut up. Peterson's first two attorneys, Fred Morelli and Gary Johnson of Aurora, Illinois, might have actually fired him, or maybe he gave them the sack. Either way, the relationship was obviously not working, because while Morelli and Johnson were representing him, Peterson went on the *Today* show and asked for a lawyer to come forward and take his case.

Peterson mentioned to host Matt Lauer—during the same appearance in which he discussed how Stacy's menstrual cycle took a toll on their marriage—that he was frightened by the prospect of funding his legal defense. "Talking to lawyers Monday night, it could cost as much as a quarter-million dollars to defend one of these cases," Peterson said. "So, basically, I'm reaching out to attorneys of America for help.

"If anybody would like to take my case and help me out here, please call," Peterson said. "Let me know what you can do for me. Help me out."

Sure enough, Peterson did get a call. It came from Chicago attorney Joel Brodsky. And in Brodsky, Peterson may have found legal counsel who enjoyed attention as much as he did—as long as the attention was not on his personal life or questionable professional actions.

Brodsky bristled when it surfaced that the Illinois Attorney Registration and Disciplinary Commission suspended his law license for three months for forging a dead man's signature to get paid. On May 8, 2001, the commission administrator filed a one-count complaint against Brodsky, alleging that he "forged a signature on bank forms in order to withdraw client funds from the bank, falsely endorsed a cashier's check issued by the bank, failed to deposit the proceeds in a separate identifiable trust account and kept the funds for his own purposes."

Later, the Illinois Supreme Court agreed with a review board that Brodsky did not commit forgery, because he did not intend to defraud anyone.

Brodsky again got bent out of shape when it came to light that in September of 2002 a SWAT team had responded to his home in the upscale Chicago suburb of Wilmette.

A report of the incident, which was classified as "mental-suicidal subject," said that Brodsky's wife, Elizabeth Brodsky, went to the police station about 6 p.m. and claimed her husband was "inside the house armed with a shotgun."

Elizabeth Brodsky later said she did not think her husband was suicidal and had no intention of conveying that to the police. She said she had merely argued with Brodsky and had gone to the police station in hopes of talking to a counselor. The police asked her if there were any guns in the house, she said, and she told them there were two. She insists she never said her husband was "armed with a shotgun," and she was very critical of the Wilmette Police Department in general.

Regardless of what Elizabeth Brodsky said at the time or five years later, the police surrounded her home and a squad of officers was sent to the Brodsky residence, dispatched through the multijurisdictional Northern Illinois Police Alarm System. Elizabeth and Joel Brodsky described this group as a SWAT team.

Joel Brodsky also said suicide was not on his mind after arguing with his wife.

"I'm in my living room watching TV," he said. "Next thing I know, I'm getting a call from a hostage negotiator."

Brodsky was taken from his home to Evanston Hospital. No one was arrested in connection with the incident.

But when his personal life was not under the microscope, Brodsky not only tolerated the media attention—he ran after it. And there was little indication that he discouraged his client from doing the same.

The pair went on the *Today* show and Brodsky appeared with some frequency on cable-network news programs. The two of them seemed to be trying to outdo one another with outrageous quotes.

Asked how Stacy, a young mother with four children to take care of and a house to keep up, would have time to carry on the adulterous affair alleged by her husband, Brodsky said, "There's always room for Jell-O." On the author of a threatening letter to Peterson, Brodsky said, "You tell me a guy who writes a letter like this wouldn't try to kill Drew?" and warned the would-be attacker that his client was a karate expert and ex-police officer. "You definitely don't know what you're getting into," the attorney declared.

Brodsky was pleased with the persona he projected on the small screen. "I can tell you, I think I do a pretty good job on TV," he said. "People have told me I do a pretty good job."

While he said he still enjoyed trying cases, he also seemed to be auditioning for a career in show business. Acknowledging that he might want to dabble in television as a second job, he mused, "It would be nice if I could mix them both."

Brodsky might have come charging in like the cavalry when Peterson implored the "attorneys of America for help," but he wasn't going to save the day for free. When I asked him if he was working the case simply for the publicity, he laughed. In an attempt to fund his legal defense and hire some private eyes to track down Stacy, Peterson launched his DefendDrew Web site in the second week of December 2007.

"For the cost of a few cups of your morning coffee, you can help to ensure that Drew can afford to support his ongoing legal defense, find his missing wife and divert any remaining funds into a trust for his children," the Web site said.

The page went on to read, "We are not asking you to decide whether or not Drew Peterson is guilty, but in the United States of America, one should be able to defend one's self without losing everything."

The site was shut down, and Peterson and Brodsky have yet to divulge how much money they raised.

They may not have made a dime, but once again Peterson succeeded in causing quite a stir, which was the last thing you would expect from a man who had become the prime suspect in one wife's disappearance and the obvious focus of police attention in another's homicide. But maybe Peterson had a feeling his situation was not so dire. Or else, after getting a taste of fame, he simply couldn't help himself.

Both Brodsky and Peterson seemed happy to be cast in virtually any light, so long as it shone on them brightly. To up the amperage of their image, they brought in Florida-based publicist Glenn Selig.

Sharon Bychowski, for one, found the notion of Peterson employing a publicist curious, if not despicable.

"Normal people don't get publicists," she said.

Selig, at least according to Peterson and Brodsky, saw dollar signs in the case of Stacy Peterson. They now wanted to get paid to talk, particularly about Peterson's days as an undercover officer with the Metropolitan Area Narcotics Squad. The restriction must have irked Peterson to some extent, because he was proud of the work he had done with the unit. He was eager to share tales of the escapades he and the other narcs got themselves into, but would not go on the record about any of it without Glenn's permission. And Glenn wanted to get paid.

Despite the involvement of Selig and whatever restrictions he may have mandated, Peterson remained glib and talkative, much like his outspoken confidant, Brodsky. Part of it was Peterson's ego, at which even he poked fun.

"I find me fascinating," he told me once, somewhat in jest. But almost everything with Peterson was a bit of a joke. It was just Drew being Drew, explained Candace Aikin.

"Like you guys see," Aikin said. "That's the way he is. He always tries to make light of a situation."

In the early days of Stacy's disappearance, Peterson was apprehensive around reporters and at times expressed his disdain for them. There was the oft-repeated television clip of Peterson, standing in his driveway, asking the press mob a curious question: "What do you get when you cross the media with a pig?"

Peterson was kind enough to provide the answer: "You get nothing, because there's some things a pig won't do."

Before long, though, Peterson warmed up to the press and showed no aversion to consorting with the swine milling around his home, wisecracking with them, and generally being pleasant and accommodating, although sometimes veering toward the bizarre.

Take, for example, the night the state police served their fourth search warrant within six weeks of Stacy vanishing. Peterson was in rare form that evening, regaling a trio of reporters who'd called on him soon after the state cops showed up at his doorstep with the paper to search his house.

Peterson addressed a wide range of subjects, from surprise that reporters had yet to pin down one of his adolescent love interests to dismissing any possibility of his appearing as a *Playgirl* magazine centerfold model. In between, he talked about not missing his career as a police officer—he'd just retired—and the lack of prospects on his romantic horizon.

"I thought you guys would be all over my eighth-grade prom date," Peterson quipped soon after I walked up to his front door. As usual, he wouldn't open the door all the way for the interview. Instead, he stood in the six-inch gap but remained there to answer questions, even though, he said, he knew this would not sit well with Brodsky.

Peterson seemed to grasp that his newfound celebrity status was not something to take for granted, and he would have to put some effort into maintaining it. When other stories threatened to push him off the front page or from the top of the hour, Peterson, with the able assistance of Brodsky, was quick to reinsert himself as the focus of attention.

Right before Christmas Eve 2007, Anu and Dignesh Solanki threatened to steal some of Peterson's time in the sun. Dignesh's wife, Anu, had driven from her home in Wheeling, Illinois, to the Des Plaines River, supposedly to dispose of a broken Hindu idol. She did not come back in a timely fashion, and the last anyone found of her was her car, left parked and running by a river dam. Fearing she had drowned, police mounted a four-day, six-mile search that involved underwater divers and helicopters. But Anu wasn't anywhere near the river.

Four days later, Anu resurfaced in Los Angeles, where she had fled with another man, just as Peterson claimed his own wife had. Despite the fact that Anu was gone only four days and Stacy, at that time, almost two months, Peterson pointed to Anu Solanki as living proof that he was telling the truth.

"This happens a lot more frequently than people are talking about," he said. "This is just another case of what happened to me happening to someone else."

After the Anu Solanki case, Brodsky issued a "demand" to prosecutors that they guarantee not to prosecute Stacy if she were ever found alive, or attempt, through a civil lawsuit, to get her to repay the cost of searching for her. Apparently this was in response to prosecutors having considered, and rejected, filing criminal charges against Anu Solanki and seeking restitution for the $250,000 search.

"We're demanding that the state's attorney come forward and state, if Stacy comes back right now, or shows herself, she will not be prosecuted or sued," Brodsky said to me.

When a representative of the state's attorney's office declined to meet his demand for this assurance, or to even recognize it, Brodsky called it a sign that they were "not as intent on getting Stacy back as they would lead us to believe. You've got a scared young girl out there who may have made a mistake and not realized the consequences." No one investigating Stacy's disappearance, however, has ever said anything about bringing charges against her.

While Brodsky's demand purported to have Stacy's best interests at heart, in late January he and Peterson called a Chicago radio show and suggested the host sponsor an on-air contest to get Peterson a date.

On January 23, Peterson and Brodsky placed an impromptu call to longtime Chicago radio personality Steve Dahl, host of a morning show on 104.3 WJMK-FM. For months, Dahl had been having a lot of fun at Peterson's expense, imitating Peterson's voice while reading the news and making up songs about his predicament. So, as Peterson later described it to Shepard Smith of Fox News, "We decided to call in and let some air out of him," keeping everything "in good nature and in good fun."

Dahl asked Peterson about a young blond woman who had reportedly left a note in his mailbox asking him to call her. The woman neglected to include her telephone number in the note, an omission Peterson described as a "blonde moment." Peterson also said that the woman had later driven by his house and blown him kisses, but nothing ever came of it.

"That's got to be encouraging, though," Dahl said. "The ladies are coming back around."

"The ladies are coming back around," agreed Peterson.

Then Brodsky piped up: Dahl should host a "Win a Date with Drew Contest."

Dahl immediately embraced the idea. "I'll absolutely do that," he said. "We'll do a Drew Peterson dating game tomorrow." Dahl said he would line up three women for Drew to interview. "Let's do it tomorrow at eight." Then he added, "But I think we're going to send a chaperone on the date, just to be on the safe side. I'm kidding! I'm kidding!"

After Peterson and Brodsky had hung up, Dahl plugged the contest to listeners: "Tomorrow, Drew Peterson dating game, 8 o'clock."

Peterson and Brodsky spent the day preparing questions for the ladies who'd be vying to go on a date with him. They approached the dating show as a comedy bit, but their questions had the ring of Peterson's recent history. Some of his questions were: "Do you need a boob job?" "Do you get PMS?" "Do you now or have you ever lived in a home that required license plates?" "Do you have any tattoos, and are they spelled correctly?"

Brodsky's contribution was, "Do you take baths or showers?" an obvious reference to Kathleen Savio, whom the audience would remember was found dead in a dry bathtub.

However, the lucky bachelorettes never got their chance with Drew. Station management, anticipating a public outcry, decided against the dating game bit the night before it was to go on the air. Peterson claimed he wasn't disappointed by the turn of events, but his dismay was apparent.

Two days later, Peterson waited outside his home in the freezing cold for nearly an hour to talk to Fox News' Shepard Smith about, he presumed, the whole radio dating game affair. Peterson thought he was in for a light interview, a break from the probing questions and cloud of suspicion, for a television piece about his sense of humor. But Smith started asking uncomfortable questions about how his children were handling their mother's disappearance and the notorious, but elusive, blue barrel.

Peterson, delighted to talk about himself at the outset of the interview, was visibly less eager to answer the more serious questions. He obliged at first, saying that he personally grieved over Stacy's disappearance but wasn't going to "hide in a corner and cry about it," and also that being a suspect in her disappearance was like having cancer: "You're just looking for that miracle cure to make it all go away." He also told Smith that his two younger children missed their mother and believed she was on vacation, but the older two boys knew she was missing.

However compliant he may have been early on, Peterson shut down the interview as soon as Shepard said, "The neighbors say they saw you carrying out a big blue barrel that would be big enough...."

"Again, again, again, Shepard, that's not what we agreed to talk about," a near-frozen Peterson said to Smith, who was playing hardball while sitting in the warmth of his New York studio.

"Oh, I didn't agree to any...any restrictions on conversation. I would never do that," Smith said unconvincingly.

"Okay, well, then I guess I got to walk away. Have a good day, Mr. Shepard," Peterson said to Mr. Smith. "It was nice talking to you."

Peterson then removed his earpiece and retreated into his garage, after soliciting assistance from the camera crew to "Unhook me, guys."

As the camera showed him walking back into his house, Smith intoned, "Well, he'll talk about the dating game, but he won't talk about the fact that the neighbors say they saw him with a large, fifty-five-gallon blue barrel, carrying it out with someone else, shortly after his wife went missing."

I followed Drew into his garage after the interview. Once he was inside and defrosting, Peterson asked me, "Did that look funny or stupid?"

I answered, in all honesty, that it was pretty funny.

Peterson was then manning the phones, taking calls from Brodsky and Selig the publicist, while his fifteen-year-old son, Thomas, watched the reactions of Smith and Geraldo Rivera on the large living room television. Rivera and Smith made rather unfavorable comments about Thomas' father while family photographs, most of which had the boy's own face and those of his siblings blurred out, flashed across the screen.

Pictures of Thomas' mother, Kathleen Savio, and Stacy Peterson, the woman who had adopted him, were also shown while commentators speculated about whether Peterson may have killed one or both women. Thomas' younger half siblings, Anthony and Lacy, played in the living room but paid little to no attention to the television. And Peterson was too wrapped up in his own televised personal drama to pay much mind to the children, at least that afternoon.

Peterson could not even escape his newfound fame when he took his children to Disney World at the end of December and into the New Year.

"The problem is, I got more stares and dirty looks," Peterson said of his failure to blend in with the crowds in the Magic Kingdom. "One guy called me Scott Peterson," the California man who is on death row after having been found guilty in 2004 of killing his wife and unborn son.

Drew Peterson might have been complaining about his notoriety, but he could not hide the pleasure he took in telling how many people recognized him.

"It was like, 'That's Drew Peterson,' and it happened a lot," he said.

Peterson traveled to New York City and Los Angeles to make television appearances. He invited *People* magazine into his backyard for a photo shoot. Whenever the whirlwind of media attention billowing about him started to subside, Brodsky conveniently brought to the press another anonymous letter detailing a Stacy sighting, or a lascivious text message from a mystery lover Peterson happened to stumble upon while looking at her old cell phone. Once Brodsky claimed he was sent a photograph snapped by a retired police officer showing a woman in Thailand who he believed just might be Stacy, even though she looked nothing at all like her.

Peterson and his attorney at times seemed to be their own worst enemies. Oddly, for all the talking they did, all the outlandish remarks and apparently unwise television appearances they made, nothing came back to haunt them. After a while, the antics of Peterson and Brodsky were the only thing keeping the pair in the public eye. Eventually it seemed as though the police and prosecutors would have liked nothing better than for the world to stop paying attention to Drew Peterson and his lawyer, if only they would let that happen.

Peterson suddenly adopting a low profile was a remote possibility. The less attention he received, the more he appeared to crave it. When the media launched its second en masse invasion of his cul-de-sac—right after the February 21 announcement that the second autopsy performed on Savio's remains concluded she was the victim of a homicide—Peterson could not contain himself entirely. At one point, he said he'd do an interview if a female television reporter, who happened to be out of earshot at the time, would put on a bikini. The spotlight had found Peterson, all right—the same way trouble always seemed to.

CHAPTER TEN

Over the course of his nearly three decades in law enforcement, Drew Peterson pulled two hitches in an undercover narcotics unit. When he was in uniform, he elected to work overnights, starting his shift when the department brass was leaving for the day. And as a sergeant, Peterson had less involvement with the public than when he was a patrolman. There he called the shots, he said, from "behind the scenes."

For a man who seemed to prefer lurking in the shadows, Peterson still couldn't avoid attracting the unwanted attention of his supervisors. But then, from the stories Peterson himself tells, he always chafed against authority. Even as a freshman football player at Willowbrook High School, he was often ordered to do extra running, wearing all of his pads, as punishment for acting up during practice. All the running he was doing convinced him that he might as well join the cross country team.

"I was always running anyway," he said. Not just that, but "I was running with all that gear on."

Free of his helmet and pads, he placed in the top five at big varsity meets. But his cross-country career was cut short his junior year, he said, when he stepped into a gopher hole and severely injured his hip.

Decades later, Peterson was a police officer and was still getting into trouble. In fact, in 1985, long before the names of Drew and Stacy Peterson were splashed across national television news shows, he was actually fired from the Bolingbrook Police Department for running an unauthorized undercover operation while working for a multijurisdictional narcotics squad. A grand jury also investigated his activities in this case, but in a pattern that would repeat itself in years to come, Peterson prevailed. He was indicted, but the charges were dropped, and he got his job back.

Instead of slowing down with age, Peterson continued to find himself in the crosshairs of internal affairs as his career with the Bolingbrook Police Department drew to a close. During his last five years or so as a cop, the department launched no fewer than three probes on Peterson. In the last one, he cashed in his chips and retired before the police chief had a chance to make good on his bid to fire him.

The swan song of Peterson's career began in July of 2002 when his third wife, Kathleen Savio, accused him of breaking into her house and holding her at knifepoint against her will. The department investigated, but nothing came of it.

In September of 2007, Peterson was suspended for eight days for his part in allowing a high-speed car chase of a stolen Hummer, which ended with the wreck of the fleeing vehicle. Department policy forbids high-speed chases for stolen vehicles, on the grounds that recapturing someone's swiped Hummer is not worth putting officers, pedestrians, and other drivers in danger of being run off the road.

No one was hurt and Peterson was not directly involved in the pursuit, but Police Chief Ray McGury suspended "like a half a dozen officers," he said, with Peterson getting the longest penalty "because he's a supervisor and I hold him to a higher standard."

Peterson didn't even know the chase was going on until the cars passed right by a restaurant where he was sitting with Stacy.

"They were discussing—he didn't get into detail what they were discussing, and I didn't need to know that,"

McGury said. "I just needed to impress upon him that you are the supervisor and you're in charge of the shift. You know you've got cars driving by you at excessive speeds, chasing a stolen car, which you know is a total violation of policy." A sergeant should know, McGury said, that if he sees a squad car rocketing down the road, "you then have to pick up the phone and call the dispatcher to find out what's going on."

Just a few weeks later, on October 29, Stacy Peterson was reported missing, bringing McGury not only more headaches but also unwanted national media attention directed at his department. The investigation into her disappearance was quickly handed off to the state police, who in the early days of their inquiry—sometime between October 29 and November 9, when Peterson was suspended without pay—developed information about Peterson that they passed back to the Bolingbrook department, prompting yet another internal probe of the volatile sergeant.

The subject of the inquiry hasn't been made public, but Bolingbrook Police Lieutenant Ken Teppel said it was unrelated to Stacy's disappearance. Teppel explained that the unspecified offense that Peterson allegedly committed while on the job could be classified as official misconduct, which is a felony. If convicted, it would cost him the roughly $6,000 monthly pension he was set to collect for the rest of his life.

Peterson resigned from his job, just shy of marking thirty years with the department. The early departure would cost him about $200 a month in pension money, but it would save him the indignity of further investigation.

McGury refused to accept his resignation; he wanted Peterson fired. He tried to force Peterson to appear before the fire and police commission, which has the authority to hire and fire personnel. On November 20, the board ruled that it was bound by law to accept Peterson's resignation and therefore declined to allow McGury to present the results of the internal affairs probe.

The outcome rankles the police chief to this day.

"I still don't think it was a valid retirement," McGury said. "I'm not an attorney. And there's absolutely— well, there's no doubt he circumvented the system so that he didn't have to stand, you know, and be charged with some things."

Maybe McGury couldn't fire Peterson, but he could try to get him arrested, and possibly stripped of his pension. He passed the fruits of the internal affairs investigation on to Will County State's Attorney James Glasgow. It apparently did not meet Glasgow's standards; no charges were brought as a result of the investigation. Peterson retired with his pension, about $70,000 a year, intact. As he had so many other times in his life, Drew Peterson got out of another scrape without suffering any real repercussions.

The end of 2007 was a trying time for Bolingbrook Police Chief Ray McGury. Drew Peterson, the department's longtime overnight sergeant, was daily fodder for television news programs up and down the dial. "Experts" on national news programs cast McGury's department in a less than favorable light, and the chief said that he had received death threats via e-mail since Sergeant Peterson's wife had disappeared.

McGury did not deserve it. For one thing, his department was not handling the investigation of Stacy Peterson's disappearance; the Illinois State Police were. Likewise, his department was not responsible for the original and, now, second investigation into the mysterious death of Kathleen Savio; that too was the state police.

Additionally, McGury did not hire Peterson, nor was he the police chief who tried and failed to fire him in 1985. McGury was not even around when Peterson and Savio were battling each other both in and out of divorce court, or when Savio turned up dead in a dry bathtub and the state police found nothing overtly peculiar about it.

No, McGury inherited Peterson when he took the job as the Bolingbrook Police Department's top man in August of 2005, smack in the middle of the scandals sparked by Peterson and his wives. It would take some time for McGury to learn the full extent of how deeply those scandals had affected the department.

In fact, until McGury suspended Peterson in September of 2007 after the high-speed chase incident, he had rarely gotten "up close and personal" with the sergeant who would draw the eyes of the world to Bolingbrook only a month or so later. It was a matter of their schedules, McGury explained. As the chief, he worked days. Peterson, the sergeant with the most seniority, was more comfortable working after dark.

"Some of these guys I don't see for six months," McGury said. "It's just the nature of the job. I leave at 5 o'clock; they come in at 5. They're getting off at 7 a.m.; I'm coming in at 7 a.m. And the only times I see them is when I visit roll call, let them know that I am still the chief, that guy that's in that office there. I do some ride-alongs occasionally when schedule allows. So I didn't see Drew."

Sometimes, McGury said, he wishes he had never seen Drew.

"There are some days, I was joking with my wife, where Captain McGury sounds a whole lot better than Chief McGury," he said.

He was Captain McGury at the Naperville, Police Department, where he worked for more than twenty years before leaving to lead the force in Bolingbrook.

Growing up on Chicago's South Side—in the Irish Catholic enclave around 103rd Street and Pulaski Avenue—McGury initially wanted to become a fireman, like his dad, but he became interested in law enforcement while attending St. Xavier University, in his same South Side neighborhood.

McGury left the neighborhood to work first for the Palos Hills Police Department, and then Naperville, when the tiny town was on the cusp of a population explosion that saw it take off to become one of the most desirable places to live in the United States. That's where he came under the influence of David Dial, a police chief who had the idea of molding his staff into future police chiefs themselves.

"The more you're around Dave, the more you kind of say, maybe being the chief of police, being the top dog, would be kind of interesting," he said. "When the Bolingbrook job came available, it was tempting only because it's in the area. I didn't have to uproot my family too much."

While the two towns share a border, the communities are quite different. Naperville, founded in 1831, boasts higher property values, a posh downtown, thriving nightlife, and pride in its traditions and history. Its downtown Riverwalk is a regional attraction. There was also the 2006 *Money* magazine article, listing the town as the second-best place to live in the United States, and other magazines and organizations have bestowed similar recognition. Bolingbrook, meanwhile, was incorporated in 1965 and has, well, a very nice shopping mall.

McGury said he knew about these differences from the beginning but still was not prepared for what awaited him in his new position.

About six months into his tenure, the superintendent of the town's public works department, along with his predecessor, were implicated in a theft scandal. Federal investigators were brought in to probe the matter, and in January of 2007, the two men, Donald Ralls and John Schwab, pleaded guilty to tax fraud. Since then, the federal investigation seems to have branched out.

"It's no secret," McGury said. "The mayor [Roger Claar] would tell you this if he sat here with you, is that the feds are looking at him."

While the theft scandal was a big enough deal to attract news coverage in nearby Chicago, it was nothing compared to the media onslaught that was unleashed after October 29, 2007, when the fourth wife of the department's overnight sergeant was reported missing.

A missing wife would have been bad enough without knowing what had befallen the previous Mrs. Peterson. As it happened, McGury did not know—he was hired more than a year after the first investigation into Kathleen

Savio's death—until he was confronted by Stacy's sister and father a day after the young woman was last seen.

"I met with Cassandra [Cales] and her father," McGury said. He had called the meeting himself and endured, he said, about "twenty minutes of them really, really being angry with me personally for allowing this to happen." Then Cassandra brought up something that McGury had never heard, causing him to cast a questioning glance over to his deputy chief, who was also at the meeting.

"She says, 'This is no different than with his third wife.' And I said, 'What do you mean, with his third wife?'" McGury said. He had heard she passed away, but he never had any idea of the circumstances and controversy surrounding her death.

"And [Cassandra] said she was obviously murdered. I said, 'Well, wait a minute. What are you talking about?' She said, 'Oh, yeah, act like you don't know.' I said, 'I'm telling you, I don't have any idea what you're talking about other than I know she is deceased. And that's how he married Stacy.'

"So then it was like an hour long getting me caught up to speed," McGury said. "After they left, I looked at my deputy chief and said, 'This would've been kind of important for me to know.' And he goes, 'You've got to understand something: A) We weren't involved in this. B) It was ruled a drowning. And we to this day never read any reports. We've never seen anything because state police did all of it.'"

That did not stop the public from slamming the entire Bolingbrook Police Department in general, and its chief in particular, even though he wasn't working in Bolingbrook during the first investigation of Savio's death. Of his twenty-seven years in law enforcement, McGury said, the first four to six weeks after Stacy Peterson disappeared were "probably the toughest." He was bombarded with hate mail and death threats.

The threats and criticism have tapered off, but whenever a Drew Peterson program airs on television, McGury sees an uptick in nasty messages. "There's a lunatic fringe out there that, you know, that's going to come out of the woodwork. My major concern was the department, trying to keep the department together, keep it on track."

While he'd doubtlessly like to keep the lunatic fringe at bay, McGury has invited federal investigators to delve into his department's handling of Peterson and Savio's domestic feud, as well as just about everything else from that time to the present day. He's turned all files over to the FBI and asked the agency to comb through everything, and the FBI has obliged.

McGury said he knows some of his staff members didn't welcome a federal investigation, but he feels it's necessary for the future well-being of the department.

"I want to know from a department standpoint what we did either on purpose or by mistake," McGury said. "One way or another I've got to get this department turned around. I have to. As long as I'm the chief, I have to do that." If the feds turn up proof of wrongdoing, he has vowed to hold people accountable

"If we screwed something up with the Peterson marriage to Stacy, I got to know that."

Besides opening his door to the feds, McGury has been up front with the public and press as well; shortly after Stacy went missing, for example, he appeared on Greta Van Susteren's Fox News show. Other police agencies have not been as forthcoming.

The state police, McGury said, "just are awful" at handling the media. He said they tried to forbid him from appearing on Van Susteren's show. "And I said, 'Last time I checked, I'm the chief of police. So you're not going to forbid me from doing anything.'"

Cooperative as he was with the press, by the end of November 2007, the police chief had had enough of the national media caravan camped out in his town, as well as the snide allusions to small-town police corruption and incompetence, and the cloud of scandal hovering over the department he had headed for a little more than two years. He also was angered by the way the veteran sergeant comported himself while in the public eye, like the time Peterson popped up in front of television cameras with the American flag bandanna tied over his face, dark sunglasses covering his eyes, and an NYPD hat situated low on his forehead.

"It's an embarrassment," McGury said of Peterson's conduct. Others in the department shared his opinion, he added.

"They're cautious, though, and they should be, in that he's only been named a suspect," the chief said. "He hasn't been charged with anything. So we can't leap to the judgment that he's responsible for the deaths of his third and now-missing fourth wife."

With all his attendant drama, Peterson may have worn on his colleagues by the end of his career, but many have said that in his heyday, he was a talented undercover narcotics officer. Peterson will tell you that himself.

"I excelled at that," he said.

While Peterson obviously enjoyed discussing his exploits as an undercover drug agent, a few months after the state police announced that he was their only suspect in the "potential homicide" of his missing wife, Peterson clammed up. He had retained the services of Glenn Selig, who, Peterson said, advised him to keep his mouth shut when asked about entertaining tales from his past. After all, there was money at stake.

"If the networks are paying for it, I can't give it away," was how Peterson put it.

Before the vow of silence, though, he'd shared a few stories with me about his undercover work on a narcotics squad he clearly loved being a part of. Oddly enough, it was during this time that Peterson found himself in the most precarious jam of his career—at least until Stacy disappeared.

Peterson took that particular hit in 1985, while working under a different chief, William Charnisky. At the time, Charnisky had loaned Peterson out to the Metropolitan Area Narcotics Squad, a drug enforcement task force based on the outskirts of nearby Joliet.

Agents in the unit were drawn from various law enforcement entitites, including the Illinois State Police, with officers assigned to the squad generally serving three years. Peterson logged five and a half years in two separate tours of duty. Peterson speaks fondly of one of his supervisors from the narcotics squad, Mike Kraft, another officer from Bolingbrook who eventually rose to the level of assistant chief of that department. Peterson was less impressed with another supervisor, Ronald Janota, who came from the ranks of the Illinois State Police to head up the squad.

"I have nothing good to say about Ron Janota, other than I feel he was truly an incompetent leader," Peterson said of the state police lieutenant colonel after both had retired from their careers in law enforcement. He eventually sued Janota and others whom he charged with harassment and trying to discredit him.

According to court documents, Peterson's problems in the Metropolitan Area Narcotics Squad started when he revealed to his supervisors that he had embarked on an unsanctioned investigation to nail Anthony "Bindy" Rock, a high-profile criminal in Joliet in the 1970s and 1980s who shared with Peterson a knack for slipping out of serious trouble, perhaps most notoriously avoiding a lengthy prison stay after his conviction in a cop-killing case. It just so happened that at the time Peterson went off on his solo pursuit of Rock, the state police had their own case going against the man, and Peterson knew it. He disclosed his after-hours investigation only after it ultimately failed.

Peterson has his own take on the matter, of course. The way he tells it, he was the victim of a petty prosecutor, Ed Petka, who was jealous of his success in undercover narcotics endeavors.

Rock had been convicted of murder, burglary and criminal damage to property in connection with a 1970 robbery of a wine-and-liquor warehouse that resulted in the slaying of Joliet Police Officer William Loscheider, one of seventeen cops participating in surveillance of the building. Loscheider was actually shot by another officer, who mistook him for one of the fleeing burglars, but Rock was convicted of murder. After a series of appeals, the state Supreme Court upheld the original conviction, but a judge gave Rock a sentence that amounted to a little more than time served. He was concurrently serving time for other convictions, so he stayed in prison another couple of years, but in all, considering the seriousness of a murder conviction in a cop-killing case, he ended up spending very little time behind bars.

"Nobody could get him," Peterson said. "The state couldn't get him. I got him."

Peterson said he nailed Rock for possession of ten thousand hits of amphetamines in November 1980. While the case ended up with a conviction, Rock beat it on appeal. But Peterson, saying he was determined to collar Rock, tried a second time in 1985.

The "investigative report" Peterson turned in on his dealings with Rock from April 28, 1985, to May 3, 1985, starts with Peterson making plans with Jerry O'Neill, the brother of his second wife, for the purpose of "purchasing cocaine from Anthony Rock."

Peterson said he hoped to lure Rock into selling him cocaine by convincing him he was a "dirty cop." In his report, Peterson said he told Rock he was "tired of watching everyone else get rich and that [he] now had an entire system set up to 'move cocaine'" and "if anybody could help him, it would be Bindy."

The whole "dirty cop" ruse, Peterson later explained to me, was why he took his ex-brother-in-law along to set Rock up. O'Neill—with whom Peterson remained close even after divorcing O'Neill's sister—was described in Peterson's report as a member in good standing of the Hell's Henchmen motorcycle gang. Peterson told me he brought O'Neill with him in hopes of appearing more genuinely criminal. (Their adversarial occupations notwithstanding, Peterson and O'Neill's friendship ended only with O'Neill's getting his face shot off in Cook County, Illinois. The man or men who gunned him down have never been brought to justice.)

A local police officer who worked in an undercover narcotics unit said enlisting one's civilian brother-in-law for assistance in a solo drug operation is highly unusual. Nonetheless, Peterson managed to set up a meeting with Rock. During this meeting, they felt each other out, and at one point played a "what if" game, each speculating on different ways one could set the other up.

One way, Rock suggested, was if the state's attorney, Petka, was granting Peterson immunity while he was behaving like a "dirty cop." Rock then asked, "Why does Petka want me so bad?" Peterson stroked Rock's ego, telling him it was because Rock was "the ultimate in criminals."

Peterson said he proposed a business arrangement with Rock in which he would buy cocaine from him in exchange for twenty percent of the front and ten percent of what was sold afterward. In his report, Peterson said he agreed but told Rock he would look for a better connection elsewhere once he was started.

Rock has seen Peterson's report and told me it was dead-on accurate, "just opposite" in terms of the business arrangement. Rock told me Peterson approached him with a plan in which Peterson would supply Rock with cocaine ripped off from his drug raids with the narcotics squad, expecting Rock to move it and surrender a percentage of his net sales. Rock told me he was not interested in Peterson's scheme. In other words, according to Rock, there was no "dirty cop" pretense at all. Peterson genuinely wanted to sell drugs through Rock; he truly was a dirty cop.

"Yeah, okay," Peterson said when told about Rock's take on his undercover operation. "That never happened, so he's got to put his spin on it."

When Chief Charnisky learned of Peterson's ploy, he went after Peterson's job.

Bolingbrook's board of fire and police commissioners found Peterson guilty of disobedience, conducting a self-assigned investigation, failure to report a bribe immediately, and official misconduct. The board fired him. Two months earlier, a grand jury had indicted Peterson on charges of official misconduct and failure to report a bribe.

Peterson blamed Petka for this, saying, "He shotgunned me."

But then the criminal charges were dropped. The special prosecutor appointed to try the case, Raymond Bolden, who later became a judge, said at the time that the charges were not provable. And in March of 1986 Peterson got his job back. Judge Edwin Grabiec ruled that the fire and police commission did not have sufficient evidence to find him guilty of the charges. Not even the chief of police could shake Peterson off the force.

Peterson responded by going on the offensive, suing Petka, who by then was an Illinois state representative; Charnisky; Janota; the town of Bolingbrook; and the fire and police commission. Peterson's lawsuit alleged the defendants met and conspired to discredit and harass him, and that they prevented further investigation of statements he reported Rock had made during their interaction, statements accusing Petka of taking kickbacks and Janota of being incompetent.

Peterson said the suit was kicked out.

"They hid behind Petka's executive immunity," he claimed.

So, after that whole flap, Charnisky was still stuck with Peterson, the cop he could not oust. History would repeat itself twenty-two years later, when Chief McGury also failed in his attempt to fire Peterson.

In the end, McGury knew the law was on Peterson's side, and whether he liked it or not, he had to let him quit. He compared fighting Peterson's resignation to throwing money away on a nuisance lawsuit.

"It becomes dollars and cents," McGury said. "Is this worth fighting for $300 an hour? Or is it worth writing this person a check for five grand and saying, 'Get out of here'?... That's why I think they looked at this and said, in the big picture, 'We need to get beyond this, move on. He wants to leave. We want him to leave. Let him leave.' I think they just wanted him gone.

"I did too. But I also wanted him to stand trial. Then one of my friends who's an attorney said, 'You got to remember something. You can't hold somebody hostage to punish them. They have the right to leave.'"

Peterson had the right to leave, and he left. But McGury predicted his former overnight sergeant would face a far worse punishment than anything handed down by the Bolingbrook fire and police commission.

"I know very well from what the state police tell me," McGury said. "If I'm a betting person, at some point they'll charge him with the murder of Kathleen Savio and that'll lead into a motive to get rid of Stacy."

Six months into the case, McGury's bet had not paid off. But the game wasn't over yet.

CHAPTER ELEVEN

The mystery surrounding Stacy Peterson consumed Roy Taylor's life after the young woman vanished in October 2007. The father of a fifteen-year-old girl and son of Sharon Bychowski, Taylor held down a house-painting job and had enough going on before that fateful fall, but none of that mattered quite as much after Stacy disappeared. Finding his mother's best friend and next-door neighbor became his major preoccupation.

"It's *the* priority," Taylor said emphatically. "The most important thing in my life: God, family and Stacy. The most important thing I have going in my life."

Almost immediately after Cassandra Cales reported Stacy missing to the police, Taylor took to the fields around her Bolingbrook home in a desperate bid to find her. He dealt with various groups such as Texas Equusearch, a search-and-rescue outfit that works on horseback and in November of 2007 joined the search for Stacy. Combing the area, however, turned up nothing, and the arrival of winter effectively halted the volunteer effort to find Stacy.

Cassandra said the police never ceased their search operations, and on at least one occasion even used jackhammers to break through ice. But the men and women who were not getting paid to look for Stacy lacked the resources—or the guidance from police—to tackle such an endeavor.

The volunteers might have had an off-season, but Taylor didn't rest. He labored through the winter months to prepare for the resumption of searches in the spring. He and his mother, along with a select group of others, organized fundraisers to offset the cost of fuel and other search necessities.

As soon as the weather warmed, Taylor's efforts were back in full swing. By late March, he was leading a team of volunteers through a swampy field near Joliet Junior College, where Stacy was taking nursing classes up until the time she vanished. It was the volunteers' first search of the year.

"Apparently it's a place police go to kind of kick back, you know, for a few hours in between," Taylor said. "They catch a lot of young people doing stuff they shouldn't."

In fact Taylor, who assumed the role of "search coordinator," said he spoke with the Illinois State Police, who provided him with promising search locations, including the field by the junior college. The locations were kept secret until the last possible moment, out of fear that if they were publicized too early, they could be compromised by someone moving the very thing the searchers hoped to find. Most volunteers didn't say it in so many words, but there was no getting around the fact that what they were looking for that last weekend in March was a dead body.

The field was also in the vicinity of the home of Scott Rossetto, with whom the police—despite the male nurse's strident denials—believed Stacy might have been romantically involved, and whom, a police source has said, Peterson might have been trying to frame for Stacy's disappearance.

Taylor was not sure Rossetto was the reason the state police sent him and his volunteers to the field.

"It was a location of their interest," Taylor said. "I believe the land there is under some kind of bank foreclosure—an old nursery. It hasn't been occupied for some time."

He conceded that Rossetto could have been part of the equation, but he emphasized that other factors went into the state police's directing volunteers down to the south end of Joliet's west side.

"We talked with [state police] about that," Taylor said. "They basically said, 'Don't think like that. Think like that but also think like this, and think like this. Don't be one track, be very open.'"

That Saturday, there were no identifiable representatives of the state police in the field. Taylor did not elaborate on the details of why they directed him to that spot, or how confident they felt about Stacy being there. It was curious, though, that the state police would set loose a group of volunteers without police supervision in an area where investigators truly believed the victim of a homicide might have been dumped. How would that conversation have gone? "Sure, we think she's in that field by the junior college. Just go out and walk all over the place and poke around with your sticks. If you find her, give us a call right away. And remember: Don't touch anything. That's real important."

It was possible, but doubtful. Then again, in light of their handling of Kathleen Savio's death, it seems nothing from the state police, as far as this particular case went, could be considered beyond the pale.

Before heading off for the Saturday search, Taylor signed up and registered about five dozen volunteers at the Bolingbrook Aquatic Center. The volunteers received a modicum of training from local emergency services and disaster agency workers—one of whom had his pistol with him—who were offering their professional guidance on their day off. Then the searchers traveled south on Interstate 55 to get down to business.

Jim Murray, clad in a red plaid jacket and armed with a walking stick, had something in common with the other volunteers trudging across the marshy ground. He did not know Stacy Peterson. He'd come out that afternoon because he was a longtime Bolingbrook resident, and since he had the time, he thought he should help.

"It's a worthy thing to do," he said. "I'm an outdoorsman. I do a lot of mountain climbing, rock climbing." He felt these attributes would be a valuable contribution to the team, along with his past experience as a volunteer to locate missing people, back when he lived in Washington State.

Murray's day job, building computers, doesn't afford him many opportunities for mountain and rock climbing. Getting outside while taking up a cause as noble as searching for a missing mother, one who might have been murdered and hidden, depriving her loved ones of closure, was too much for a man like Murray to pass up.

"I have a very boring life right now," he said. "I like to do a lot of outdoors [activities], bike riding. Any opportunity I get to help in a situation like this—I mean, I'm a Bolingbrook resident. Anybody who has spare time on their hands and they live anywhere near here and they don't come out and help, I think they need to check their priorities."

Another volunteer, Marie Galluzzi, knew Stacy and her kin about as well as Murray did.

"I'm just out here to help," said Galluzzi, who was taking part in her first Stacy Peterson search. "Hopefully help them put an end to their hurting."

A neighbor had accompanied her from Chicago down to Bolingbrook and Joliet. The neighbor explained that the search was a way for her to put off doing her chemistry homework, a reason that fell a bit short of Murray's more idealistic motivations.

The volunteers were visibly eager to get under way. Even before Taylor provided instructions and let them loose, a pair of young women made a discovery of sorts.

"Okay, there's underwear," one said breathlessly to the other as she pointed to a pair of soiled, once-white briefs lying in the leaves along a path. No one seemed too interested in the young woman's find, and she cried out, "Does anybody want to look at the underwear?"

Some of her fellow volunteers did want to look. One prodded the underwear with a walking stick, and one of the search-and-rescue workers gave the garment a good visual going-over. A group of volunteers discussed for several minutes the possibility that the underwear might have something to do with Stacy Peterson, but ultimately the general consensus was that, no, it probably did not.

Soon after this, two search-and-rescue workers happened upon and examined a filthy bedsheet spotted not far from the underwear. The sheet was of such potential significance that they ordered a television cameraman to stop filming and forbade photographers to snap any more pictures, apparently out of security concerns. There was even talk of saving the sheet for the state police.

After those two early discoveries, the search moved on. The crew in the field was a colorful bunch, in a literal sense. A good number sported orange, yellow and pink Stacy Peterson "missing person" T-shirts, complete with her photograph, the number of the telephone tip line and mention of the $25,000 reward offered for information leading to her return. These volunteers were very visible as they plodded across the sodden ground, armed with broomsticks, ski poles, or whatever other implement they chose to use in stabbing and beating the brush and soil that could be concealing Stacy.

Rotting pieces of plywood were lifted and looked under, manhole covers were removed to see if anything lay inside, and the tall, dead grass was tramped over. But Stacy Peterson could have been there all along, and it is still conceivable the searchers would have missed her.

The organizers tried to keep volunteers in a straight formation as they marched across the fields, but the line kept disintegrating within a matter of steps. Bolting rabbits startled some searchers; others drifted into small groups. A sense of distraction seemed to prevail, as volunteers at times appeared to wander around on their own. And some of the searchers did not seem to be doing much searching at all. As one volunteer grumbled, "With all due respect to the folks who came out to search, they've got a smoke in one hand and a cell phone in the other. Are you out here to search or to talk to your friends?"

The man who made this remark was not a popular one. In fact, several of his colleagues tried with great fervor to convince one of the search-and-rescue workers to have him removed. They claimed the man had shown up drunk to a search in the fall of 2007 and struck another volunteer. The unwanted man hung around for a while, but eventually departed early.

Despite their differences and failure to turn up any real sign of Stacy, at the conclusion of the first day's search, Taylor was nevertheless encouraged.

"We did real good today," he said, after the volunteers wrapped things up and he took a break to get a bite to eat in a nearby Burger King before going back out with the diehards to search some more. "[This] is much better than what we have dealt with in the past. It's tenfold what it was."

The volunteers shared his enthusiasm, he said, and he took heart that the operation had gotten off to a good beginning.

"The people obviously are a little happier that it's more fluid," he said. "I think they're more reassured that we have a better format. We have an emergency-management presence. We're all working together, I think, a little better than we have in the past. We're coordinated better."

One conspicuous absence among the men and women in the field was Drew Peterson himself. Neighbors and friends said he had recently returned to town after taking his children to a Wisconsin water park during their spring break from school.

He'd gotten back in time to lend a hand, but Peterson was not interested. The day before Taylor's first search of the spring was to take place, Peterson stood in the front doorway of his home. Asked whether he would be participating, he laughed. When questioned about what he thought of the many men and women sacrificing their time and effort to look for his missing wife's body, he said, "Go for it," and chuckled again. He also mocked Taylor, calling him "Sharon's goofy son Elroy" and "Opie." Stacy, in fact, couldn't stand Taylor, Peterson told me a few days after the search. This dislike stemmed somehow from an episode in which Sharon's son offered to paint the Petersons' house, and the couple declined.

Peterson's attorney had a more expansive response than Peterson to the dozens of men and women willing to give up their weekends to look for his client's wife.

"God bless them," Brodsky said when I interviewed him, three days before the search, for an article published in *The Herald News*.

"This is America," he went on. "I can't stop them from wasting their time. They can search every bush, pond and river in the state of Illinois if that makes them happy."

As far as lawyer and client were concerned, their stance was: What was the point of walking around in the weeds and mud when Drew Peterson had said from the very beginning that his wife was alive and well? How many times was he going to have to tell everyone that she had run off with another man? He was the victim here, the one abandoned and left to take care of four children by himself.

And Stacy didn't leave Peterson to go start a new life in some desolate Joliet field. She was Bahamas bound, Peterson had reportedly claimed. Then again, there was that person who claimed to have sighted the young woman in Kentucky. And there was the letter placing Stacy in a Peoria, Illinois supermarket, looking pregnant. Perhaps she was in Thailand, Brodsky and Peterson stipulated to the media, as one photo demonstrated. Of course, no one else believed it was Stacy in the photograph, even though the shot supposedly came from somebody as reliable as a retired cop—somebody just like Drew.

Wherever Stacy was, it was not a field in Joliet. It was not a field anywhere. It was somewhere warm and tropical like the Bahamas or Thailand, maybe Peoria or Kentucky, but definitely with another man.

"If they would just consider," Brodsky suggested in that same interview, "as a possibility that she started her life over overseas, Drew would certainly contribute to that [search] effort."

Stacy's sister Cassandra did not buy—has never bought—Peterson's story about his wife running off with another man.

"Drew Peterson believes that my sister left and that we should be searching in other towns, and Jamaica and Thailand," Cassandra said during a press conference to announce the resumption of the searches for Stacy. "My sister did not leave willingly."

To think otherwise, most would say, is delusional. Stacy is no more in Thailand or Jamaica than she is on the moon. But to think she is in a nearby field, one the state police invited inexperienced volunteers to attack on their own, seems equally implausible.

At least the volunteers could say they were trying to help. Drew Peterson, on the other hand, must have had more important things to do. But for all their trying, for all their good intentions, the volunteers walking around that field were not accomplishing much. Even among their ranks, there was no shortage of criticism. Two questioned how the searchers would react upon seeing a decomposed corpse that had been lying out in the elements for five months.

"Have any of these people ever seen a dead body?" asked the woman, who did not want to be identified but said her line of work exposes her to deceased people. "Do they even know what a body's going to look like after all this time?"

It was probably safe to assume that few of the volunteers meandering around the marshland close to Joliet Junior College had been anywhere near decomposing human remains. God only knows what their reaction might have been had they actually stumbled upon them. But on the first search of the spring after Stacy disappeared, that did not happen. It did not happen the next day either. With each passing day, it seemed less likely that it ever would.

However fruitless their efforts seemed, the volunteers were not dismayed in the slightest by the prospect of returning to duty. As far as Roy Taylor was concerned, he was never going to give up.

"This is my life," he once told me. "This is the most important thing I've done in my life."

CHAPTER TWELVE

Hours after anyone last spoke to Drew Peterson's fourth wife, the Red Sox won the World Series and third baseman Mike Lowell was named most valuable player. Nearly four months later, on the day state officials changed Kathleen Savio's four-year-old accidental drowning verdict to a homicide, Hillary Rodham Clinton and Barack Obama were facing off in the increasingly rancorous Texas Democratic primary.

Back in Bolingbrook, Drew Peterson was hunkered down in his home on Pheasant Chase Court. He had never played in a World Series, and he wasn't running for office, but over the course of the last months of 2007 and the first few of 2008, he occasionally dominated the news cycle in a way that any professional athlete or campaign strategist would envy.

Things appeared grim for Peterson: the Illinois State Police went out on a limb within the first two weeks of Stacy's disappearance and boldly classified her case a "potential homicide," naming Peterson a suspect. The once-closed investigation into Savio's death also was reopened. Yet despite all the labeling and classifying by the state police, all of their contradicting, accusing and probing, Peterson remained insolent and self-confident.

"No, I've never, ever seen anything like this," said psychologist Philip Bonelli, referring to Drew Peterson's

public persona. Bonelli, like many residents of Illinois, has
followed the case with acute interest.

Bonelli's office on quiet West Oak Street in Plainfield
is about fifteen minutes from Peterson's front door. He
opened his practice in 1979 and works in the same town as
Illinois' other infamous "abandoned" husband—Craig
Stebic, the pipe fitter whose estranged wife disappeared
about six months before Stacy went missing. The
appearance of headline-hogging Drew Peterson, with his
attention-grabbing antics and double the number of wives
who may have come to unnatural ends, was the best thing
that could ever happen to Stebic, a low-key workingman
who promptly got shoved off the front page once his erratic
neighbor from Bolingbrook had a taste of fame.

One of the main tenets of psychology is that
diagnosing a patient without the chance to evaluate him
directly makes assessment challenging. Before offering an
opinion, any credible mental health professional asked to
comment on, say, a celebrity acting bizarrely in public or a
suspect in a tabloid-murder case will offer the important
caveat, "This person is not a client of mine." However,
evaluating a nonclient in the news offers some advantages
over a traditional client whom the therapist sees privately in
his or her office. It provides the rare opportunity to observe
the client in the outside world, interacting with others, his
full range of emotions on display, and how he handles
situations that cannot possibly be duplicated in a counseling
session. There is another advantage to evaluating a person
based on his documented public behavior rather than on his
account of events in a forty-five-minute session: The
psychologist can view the behavior first hand, rather than
have to interpret through a prism of whatever defenses,
agendas, and distortions the client may have.

I think that his pattern of deception
in relationships and then further deception
to cover up the deception certainly makes him
a less credible individual. It makes one
wonder why he has to lie about so many

important things. Is he capable of a
relationship? And, if he's not capable of any
kind of emotionally available relationship,
then one wonders if this person can have any
kind of attachment, or bonds, to others, if all
are objects to be manipulated.

The above was spoken by psychologist and *Raising a Secure Child* author Zeynep Biringen and taken from a Court TV news transcript. Here Biringen is talking about a man named Peterson, but not Drew; she is talking about convicted murderer Scott Peterson in an interview conducted in September of 2004.

In the same interview, Biringen states unequivocally that Scott Peterson has antisocial personality disorder, the preferred mental health term used to describe people commonly called sociopaths. Other psychologists, on television and in print media, agreed with Biringen's diagnosis of Scott Peterson. So perhaps both Scott and Drew share something besides a last name and media notoriety.

The World Health Organization (WHO) defines a personality disorder as: "Deeply ingrained and enduring behavior patterns, manifesting themselves as inflexible responses to a broad range of personal and social situations.... They represent either extreme or significant deviations from the way the average individual or a given culture perceives, thinks, feels and particularly relates to others.... Such behavior patterns tend to be stable and to encompass multiple domains of behavior and psychological functioning."

There are ten types of personality disorders listed in the most recent revision of the *Diagnostic and Statistical Manual of Mental Disorders* (*DSM-IV*), the bible of the psychiatric profession. These range from conditions such as obsessive-compulsive personality disorder and dependence personality disorder to the more severe and threatening antisocial personality disorder.

Bonelli, a licensed clinical psychologist, provides professional consultation for couples, families and individuals. He has never met Drew Peterson, but from following his behavior in the media, he felt confident offering his opinions on the notorious police sergeant.

"His cockiness is the thing that stands out to me," said Bonelli. "I've seen him as being almost belligerently cocky, where he wants to antagonize anyone who might have any negative responses to him.

"I thought the epitome of his cockiness came out...when he solicited that divorce attorney from Chicago, saying that he'd like to have drinks with her and talk about a divorce," Bonelli said, referring to an aside Peterson made about *Playboy* pinup and Chicago lawyer Corri Fetman, well-known locally for her "Life's short. Get a divorce." ad campaign.

Peterson told me he might be interested in retaining Fetman to initiate divorce proceedings against Stacy, who at the time had been missing for more than three months. While the forty-four-year-old Fetman might be a little long in the tooth for Peterson's taste—considering his four wives got successively younger and the last one was a teenager— the lonely stay-at-home dad indicated he would be interested in something more than just a professional relationship with the busty attorney. "If she wants to go out for drinks, give me a call," Peterson said.

It is, of course, possible that Peterson has nothing to hide, and that Stacy did in fact run off with a secret lover to indulge in an adulterous affair. Even if she did, Bonelli said, it would likely not weigh heavily on Peterson's mind. That's the way it is with antisocial personality disorder, he said, and he sees a strong sociopathic streak in Peterson.

In Bonelli's professional opinion, Peterson's behavior both past and present strongly conforms to a diagnosis of antisocial personality disorder. There are seven criteria for the disorder, which the American Psychiatric Association defines as follows:

• Lack of remorse, as indicated by being indifferent to or rationalizing having hurt, mistreated, or stolen from another.
• Failure to conform to social norms with respect to lawful behaviors as indicated by repeatedly performing acts that are grounds for arrest.
• Deceitfulness, as indicated by repeatedly lying, use of aliases, or conning others for personal profit or pleasure.
• Impulsivity or failure to plan ahead.
• Irritability and aggressiveness, as indicated by repeated physical fights or assaults.
• Reckless disregard for the safety of self or others.
• Consistent irresponsibility, as indicated by repeated failure to sustain consistent work behavior or honor financial obligations.

A person with three or more of the seven is considered a likely candidate. Peterson shows a strong possibility of possessing at least five.

Lack of remorse. For a man who maintained that his young wife ran off on him, leaving him in the lurch with four kids, two of whom had already lost a mother once in their young lives, he didn't seem terribly distraught. If he ever seriously searched for Stacy, there's no evidence of it. While the army of television cameras at his house often annoyed him, he basked in the attention as well—joking with reporters, flying to New York City a couple of times to tape television appearances, even hiring a publicist so that he could profit from his sought-after presence instead of giving away access to Drew Peterson for free.

He and his attorney, Joel Brodsky, also had a great time joking around with Chicago radio host Steve Dahl about the aborted "Win a Date with Drew Peterson" contest. Peterson was clearly disappointed when the radio station canceled the dating game, although he said he wasn't.

Irritability and aggressiveness. Friends and family of three of Peterson's four wives say he was

controlling, threatening, or outright abusive to the women.
Savio seemed especially terrified of him; she wrote in a letter
to an assistant state's attorney that "several times" during
their marriage she had ended up in the emergency room as a
result of their fights, and that after they divorced, Peterson
once broke into her house and held a knife to her neck.

His irritability manifested itself in other ways.
Instead of supporting his grief-stricken wife at the funeral of
Stacy's beloved half sister, Tina Ryan, Peterson supposedly
turned to Stacy and asked her point-blank if she were
"fucking" Ryan's equally grief-stricken husband. He walked
away from a television interview with Shepard Smith when
the Fox News personality started asking him questions
about the blue barrel and how his children were faring
without their mother. Another time, he turned his own video
camera onto the press hordes crowding his driveway.

Reckless disregard for the safety of others. If
the abuse allegations spelled out in Savio's letter to a Will
County assistant state's attorney are true, as well as the
many charges made by Savio and Stacy's family, Peterson's
last two wives certainly felt that Peterson threatened their
safety. "[H]is next step is to take my children away," Savio
wrote in the letter. "Or kill me instead." His second wife,
Vicki Connolly, also has claimed Peterson said he could kill
her and make it look like an accident, a threat Peterson
has denied.

*Repeatedly performing acts that are grounds
for arrest*. For his renegade operation against career-
criminal Anthony "Bindy" Rock, in which he presented
himself as a dirty cop who wanted to set up a drug-selling
operation, he was fired from his job and indicted on charges
of official misconduct and failure to report a bribe. The
charges were eventually dropped and Peterson got his job
back. In 2007, he was suspended from the police force for
eight days for his role in allowing a high-speed chase,
against department policy. Shortly after Stacy disappeared,
Peterson was the subject of yet another internal
investigation, on what charge the department has not said,

other than to explain that by committing the offense, Peterson would be guilty of official misconduct, which is a felony. Peterson avoided further investigation by retiring.

And certainly, if true, breaking into his ex-wife's house and holding a knife to her neck would be grounds for arrest. (Bolingbrook police investigated that allegation; nothing ever came from it.)

Deceitfulness. Peterson admits that he cheated on each of his first three wives. When cheating on Kathleen, he was so bold as to bring Stacy to his basement for sex while his wife and their sons slept upstairs. Then, after Kathleen died, he broke out a previously unknown and hardly official-looking will—a will that conveniently named his uncle as executor and left everything to Peterson.

Of course, counterarguments could be made on each point. You have to think like a criminal to catch a criminal. No charges against Peterson ever stuck, and he'd never been charged with anything in connection with domestic disputes involving his wives. In regards to the media, he was just dishing back what they heaped on him. Who wouldn't walk away from Shepard Smith when he started asking jerky questions? Anyway, Peterson was nothing but polite, saying, "Have a good day, Mr. Shepard. It was nice talking to you."

And the affairs? At least he had owned up to them, even if it sounded more like bragging than painful self-reflection. The will stood up in court. The radio show was all in good fun. If his last wife really had run off with another guy, why should he be the remorseful one?

None of these arguments would likely sway Bonelli, who has found the totality of Peterson's behavior very telling not only in providing insight into his personality but in revealing what fate Stacy met, and whether there was any basis for the slim hope she might still be alive somewhere.

"He's so self-centered. And he wouldn't be [acting as he did] if he really believed Stacy were still alive," Bonelli said, "because then she obviously would hear about this.

"Sure, if she's alive, she knows about it," he continued. "And she's going to be angry. And she's going to, sooner or later, check in. I don't care if she is off with someone else, the dude from wherever. This is enough crap to get her angry, and she'd respond to it. There's no response. Therefore, there's no Stacy. Therefore Drew can keep going and going and going and just play this egocentric game."

Whatever happened to Stacy, and regardless of whether Savio accidentally drowned in her tub, as the state police said in 2004, or if she died by the hand of another, as a forensic pathologist said four years later, Peterson's egocentric game was a dangerous one. Public opinion and political pressure were undeniable forces pulling the authorities to press charges against him, and the possibility of the police descending on his home and carting him off to jail was very real. But Peterson continued to make public appearances, banter with the press, and stick to the increasingly absurd story that his wife took off and was gallivanting around some tropical locale with another man.

Afflicting those people who, in basic terms, are hostile to society, antisocial personality disorder is believed to manifest itself in a lack of feelings or concern for the losses, pain, and suffering of victims; a tendency to be unconcerned, dispassionate, coldhearted, and unempathic, usually demonstrated by a disdain for one's victims, Bonelli explained.

"You got it. He's having fun with this. Sociopaths do that, they have fun with tragedy because they don't feel a sense of guilt," Bonelli said. "Anyone who is not sociopathic wouldn't be having fun with his wife's death and disappearance.

"It's a game. It's such a damn game to him," Bonelli continued. "He's having too much fun." Of what an antisocial personality might be thinking in such a situation, Bonelli offers, "Everything's okay, because I did it. It's okay for me."

Then there's Peterson's inclination towards deceit. He is most proud of the time he spent as an undercover narcotics officer, a calling steeped in subterfuge and duplicity.

Undercover officers "have to be deceitful," Bonelli said. "And I think they learn how to slide a lot and to avoid issues, avoid being singled out. Their identity to being an undercover cop, they have to be sly."

Diane Wetendorf, an advocate, trainer and consultant based in Arlington Heights, Illinois, and specializing in police-perpetrated domestic violence, took this a step further.

Police officers, particularly ones working undercover, "know, number one, how to lie well."

They also know, through their training, the best way to testify in court, she said. They only answer the questions, sticking strictly to facts, whereas "other defendants want to fill in," Wetendorf said. "Cops are very savvy about that. It's what they say. It's how they say it. It's what they don't say. They know what to omit."

Wetendorf created the program Spousal Abuse By Law Enforcement in 1996, which provided specialized counseling as well as legal and advocacy services for victims of officer-involved domestic violence. Wetendorf worked collaboratively with police departments to develop policies, provided advocacy to law enforcement institutions nationwide, trained community advocates, and provided thousands of hours of individual and group counseling. She is also an author and consultant.

On her Battered Women's Justice Project blog, Wetendorf references the Stacy Peterson case:

"Media coverage on the disappearance of Stacy Peterson has been remiss in its failure to highlight former Sergeant Peterson's profession as a law enforcement officer. Although most reports have noted his profession there has been no analysis addressing his law enforcement experience as a significant aspect of his emerging profile as a serial abuser."

Wetendorf noted the high-profile case of, among others, Bobby Cutts Jr., an Ohio police officer who in February 2008 was sentenced to life in prison for murdering his pregnant girlfriend. "Too often, police departments deny that police-perpetrated domestic violence is a problem," Wetendorf said. "After every exposure, they assure us that the perpetrator is a 'bad apple' and that the department 'had no idea' that the officer posed a lethal threat to the victim.

"It is time that we acknowledge this problem and recognize the fact that officers who batter can be highly skilled at abuse. Officers have professional training in tactics of manipulation, intimidation, coercion, and the use of physical force, which makes them among the most dangerous abusers. Their knowledge of how the criminal justice system operates enables them to use that system to their advantage and to successfully avoid accountability for their actions."

Wetendorf said Peterson fits all of her criteria for an abusive husband working in law enforcement. Even if it's determined that he had something to do with both Kathleen's death and Stacy's disappearance, she finds nothing particularly special about him. "There are thousands of them," Wetendorf said. "Drew just happened to make the paper, for whatever reason. There's nothing different about Peterson, except he's a little more of a ham."

Wetendorf did concede that, while she was not surprised by the methods he has been accused of using to control his last two wives, some of his antics on the nightly news, and his quotes in the papers, have left her baffled.

"I don't know what the hell's going on there," she said.

Bonelli, on the other hand, maintains that he knows exactly what the hell's going on there.

"He's feeding his ego," Bonelli said. "And this is where the arrogance and the cockiness that I spoke of at first comes right into it. He's feeding his ego. And he thinks he's not ever going to be at all caught, punished, anything. So he can get away with this."

Even when things weren't going Peterson's way, the pressure did not seem to get to him. In February 2008, soon after a forensic pathologist called Savio's death a homicide, Peterson and Brodsky were jetting back to New York City for another turn on the *Today* show. It was the third time he had appeared on the show, and this time, Peterson's demeanor was markedly more subdued.

He allowed a crew from Greta Van Susteren's program to film inside his house, following him around as he carried out his daily routine. The camera caught him performing such mundane tasks as making sandwiches for his children and taking the younger ones grocery shopping for the week's food. He bemoaned his high weekly grocery bill, but said he was willing to pay the freight, so long as it meant he would be able to prepare healthy meals for his family. Apparently, allowing Van Susteren's show to broadcast his everyday life with his family was all part of Peterson's selling the world on the notion that he possessed a softer side. His effort was less than successful, however, and Peterson later told me he was a bit put off by the public criticism he received. Even when he was comporting himself in a sensitive and responsible manner, a disappointed Peterson complained, he could not convince the whole world that he was, at heart, a decent guy. But then, Peterson had a good four months of public image to repair.

Before this attempt to appear sensitive and soft-spoken, Bonelli found Peterson's media appearances "not consistent with the realities.

"His expressions in [an interview]—he smirked. He was not real comfortable, which implied lying," Bonelli said. "His eyes, he kept shifting. He could not keep a gaze, and that is also indicative of tremendous discomfort and lying. I've talked to you, Joe, and I look you straight in the eye, because I'm confident and comfortable. In those interviews I saw coverage of, he was all over the place. And he wasn't on the interviewer. He was looking down. Looking down is always an indication of the lying thing. When you're asked a question, and you know, you don't know the answer, you look up. When you're trying to avoid something, you look down."

Antisocial personality disorder is three times as prevalent among men as it is among women. It is widely accepted that the roots of the disorder begin in childhood and that family dynamics play an influential part. Beyond Peterson's upbringing, which was detailed in a November

2007 *People* magazine article, his choice of friends in adult life offers some support to the belief that he suffers from the personality disorder. Not surprisingly, antisocial children tend to be rejected by other children. They tend to gravitate toward other poorly socialized children who are also outsiders, although even these friendships tend to be characterized by a weak bond. As the men in Drew Peterson's orbit were introduced to viewers courtesy of Greta, Nancy Grace and Geraldo, many understandably asked, "Where does Drew find these people?" Indeed the group is a sketchy bunch, and one defined by an ambivalent relationship with the center of the ring himself. There's Tom Morphey, who has reportedly battled alcoholism and regular unemployment his entire life, who reportedly leaned on his cop stepbrother for jobs and furniture. Ric Mims sold out his "good friend" to the *National Enquirer* and used his short-lived tabloid television fame to launch www.RichardMims.com. Drew's one remaining public ally appears to be Steve Carcerano, the neighbor with whom he discovered Kathleen's body. That loyalty, however, may soon be tested as well: Carcerano is seeking a lucrative book deal of his own.

The many pundits, psychologists, and online chat rooms indulging in speculation about Peterson's pathology didn't deter Peterson from turning to a member of the mental health profession to rally to his defense.

"Renowned Psychotherapist Defends Care of Drew Peterson's Children" trumpeted the press release issued by Peterson's publicist, Glenn Selig. Selig's company Web site, www.ThePublicityAgency.com, lists Peterson as a client, along with his attorney, Brodsky; "CarolAnn, Fitness Expert"; and Harper Realty of Tampa.

The "renown" of this psychotherapist, Daniel Budenz, is arguable to say the least. Budenz, a certified alcohol and drug counselor, bought a bar at one point, although he was denied the liquor license. His daughter eventually took over the property after her application for the license was approved. Selig's press release quoted Budenz at length, while noting that the psychotherapist "was friends with Peterson twenty years ago and recently reconnected."

Budenz said he got to know Peterson when they were both teenagers working at a Burger King. The pair shared interests, he said, including karate and flying.

"He had this very playful character, very sharp," Budenz said.

The two lost touch as they aged, although Budenz said he did attend the wedding of Peterson and his first wife, Carol Hamilton. He and Peterson hooked up again after Budenz saw his old pal on television discussing Stacy's disappearance.

"I figured I'd give him a call and tease him, that you're having problems with your relationship," Budenz said. Realizing the gravity of the situation, Budenz offered to lend a hand. He said he was most concerned about Peterson's kids.

"The Peterson children are caught in the middle of dueling family members and a huge media frenzy," Dr. Dan said in the press release. "The family has had to wake up at four in the morning to the roar of media generators, climb over the back fence to attend school and then hear the accusations against their dad on TV."

Despite dealing with all this adversity, Peterson was doing a fine job with the children, the statement said.

"From what I see, Drew and the outside help he's hired to help care for the children are doing a great job," Budenz's release claims.

Budenz got a chance to observe the children up close, as Peterson and his brood stayed with him at his home during their trip to Disney World during the winter break.

"We lived together with the kids," he said. "They're fine. They're adjusted."

"Stacy and Drew have done a very fine job," Budenz said, adding, "I'm not saying everything's perfect. No family is ever perfect."

"Drew is a very attentive father," Budenz's press release read. "The two oldest sons clearly understand what is happening—one is a police officer. The two teens are equally aware and are extremely helpful, wonderful,

motivated young men who stand by their dad and help
Drew with the youngest children."

He pointed out that Thomas, the older of the two
sons Peterson fathered with Savio, who was fourteen when
Stacy disappeared, was "number one in a class of more than
twelve hundred, academically."

Budenz's ringing endorsement of Peterson's
parenting skills makes no mention of the potential impact
on the children of growing up without their mothers, or of
their father's regular bragging of meeting women in bars or
of his gamely agreeing to participate in the aborted radio
dating contest. Perhaps his two youngest, Anthony, nearly
five when Dr. Dan made his way into Drew's drama, and
Lacy, three, could be sheltered from their father's cavalier
attitude toward the fate of his last two wives. However, for
the sake of Peterson's two school-aged sons, Kristopher and
Thomas, one might wish their father would exercise a little
restraint.

Nearly four months after Stacy vanished, Peterson
was still telling Anthony and Lacy that their mother was on
a "vacation." One had to wonder how long he was going to,
or would be able to, keep up this story. But, at least
according to Budenz, Peterson was doing something right.

"The three- and four-year-olds are physically and
emotionally vibrant and are well parented by Drew and the
older family members," he is quoted as saying in the press
release. "These children are in great hands."

And lying to the youngest two was "extremely
appropriate," as well.

"Drew told them, 'Mom is on vacation,'" he said.
"They don't question it.

"When the time is right to introduce more
information, we certainly will."

Bonelli sharply disagrees with this approach.

"Drew Peterson is not a child psychologist," he said
and questioned the effect that lying to the children would
have in the long run. Eventually, they're going to start
asking when Mom's vacation will end and when she'll come
home.

"What is he going to tell them? She's dead? She ran away? If you're a normal person, you tell them when you know they're not coming home. If you're Drew Peterson, you tell them anything that makes Drew Peterson feel good."

Because, Bonelli said, everything Peterson does is about Peterson.

"If Drew Peterson has an addiction, it is an addiction to power and attention," he said. "These things are driving him. And he feels he has power because he's really, in a sense, manipulating the whole country. I'd love to see [*America's Most Wanted* host] John Walsh get a hold of him. Face to face, wouldn't you love to see John Walsh and Drew Peterson go at it?"

As far as Savio's sons, Kristopher and Thomas, Bonelli believes they may not be handling matters as well as Peterson and his posse are letting on.

"I have to think that they're [Peterson's sons are] devastated," he said. "But they may have just drawn within themselves. But I can't tell you because I've never seen them. I would speculate that there's a good possibility that they've just become so withdrawn. I cannot contemplate them having a normal teenage life."

While Bonelli has not had the opportunity to observe the two teenage boys, he says he knows the correct way for their father to handle their situation.

"Whether [Stacy] ran away or is dead, if you're going to go through any kind of grief process, you've got to go through a lot of anger. Anger is necessary to get through any kind of grieving process.

"Anger towards her, anger towards him, anger towards his sister, anger towards school. Just anger, anger, lots of anger," Bonelli said. "Doing grief counseling is enabling the person to express the anger and then deal with it, because that's such a necessary process."

Budenz fired a warning shot at Bonelli and others who would dare make a psychological evaluation of his old friend without spending a significant amount of time with him, much less even meeting him.

"I have one word for that, especially for the professionals: malpractice," he said.

Besides, Budenz said, just watching Drew from the outside, observing his playful and often condescending facade, is no measure of the man he once worked with at Burger King.

"Drew has been bombarded for four months now," he said. "He will play games and play tricks on the interviewer. That's his personality.

"And that's what the media is seeing," Budenz said of what he termed Peterson's outsized "Chicago style" personality. "I don't think the media is seeing the kids."

Budenz also cautioned the public to keep an open mind about Peterson.

"Americans like to lock people up," he said. "We have people who are retarded, who have severe alcohol and drug problems, and we lock them up. We don't treat them."

Budenz also pointed out, "There are a lot of people who are locked up who didn't really do it."

Of course, there are also a lot of people who aren't locked up who really did do it.

"You know, I can't sit here and tell you what happened to her," Bonelli said in our interview. "I don't think anyone can. My gut feeling is that she's dead. He's not waiting for her to come home. He's just waiting for this whole thing to blow over. And start romancing number five."

CHAPTER THIRTEEN

When the volunteer searchers resumed their efforts the last weekend of March 2008, it seemed like Stacy Peterson had been missing not five months but forever. Since November 9, 2007, when state police announced that her husband was a suspect in her disappearance and the state's attorney announced that he was ordering Kathleen Savio's body to be exhumed for another look, no one from the criminal justice system had said much of substance regarding either case.

About the only development that broke this dry spell was the announcement in February 2008 that, according to forensic pathologist Larry Blum, Savio's death had been a homicide, not an accident.

How Blum determined this was a mystery, because Will County State's Attorney James Glasgow refused to release the report of the do-over autopsy. For all the public knew, when Blum examined Savio's exhumed corpse he found a knife stuck in her back that the state police and first forensic pathologist failed to notice in 2004. Realistically, though, little if anything is likely to have changed regarding the circumstances surrounding her death. The thing that did change, the reason that Savio's death was reexamined in the first place, was that Drew Peterson's next wife vanished.

One might think that Glasgow's limited release of Blum's findings, on top of Peterson being the only suspect in Stacy's disappearance, was a damning development for her husband. Peterson's frequent and sometimes cocky media appearances hadn't helped to dampen the public outcry that he obviously had something to do with the death of one wife and probable death of another. The months dragged on and yet he remained a free man, fueling much speculation about why this was. Were the boys in blue protecting one of their own? Were the state police incompetent? Or did Peterson, as a savvy ex-cop, know how to get away with murder?

One attorney who has worked both sides of the street in criminal law—as a prosecutor and as a defense attorney—had a different, less sensational take: Mainly, the case against Peterson was a tough one to try.

"The biggest problem with the fourth wife is they simply don't have a body," said Chuck Bretz, one of the premier criminal defense attorneys in Will County. His courtroom experience is not limited to defending the accused; he was a Will County assistant state's attorney from 1982 to 1986 and the first assistant state's attorney—under Glasgow—from 1992 to 1994.

Without a body, Bretz said, there is no scientific evidence to work with, no proof anyone was in fact killed.

"There's a lot of conjecture," he said. "There's marital problems. She's getting ready to leave. 'If anything happens, look at my husband.' As far as she's concerned, although it's possible to prosecute a case without a body, certainly it's the exception and not the rule."

Bretz himself, however, was involved with such an exception. While a prosecutor, he brought a murder charge in 1993 against Gilbert Bernal in connection with the December 1988 disappearance of his wife, Joan.

There was no body, but Bretz did have an eyewitness who would testify to observing Bernal battering his wife and inflicting what could have been fatal injuries.

"There was no other physical evidence forthcoming," Bretz said. "From the [witness'] description, it was apparent that there were no other witnesses."

Joan Bernal also supposedly told a relative her husband threatened that he could kill her, stuff her in a barrel and hide her where she would not be found. And Gilbert Bernal reportedly bought two barrels shortly before the disappearance; afterward, only one barrel was still in his garage. Unfortunately, neither the second barrel nor Joan Bernal was ever found, and almost a year later, soon after Bretz resigned from his post in the state's attorney's office, the charges against Bernal were dropped.

Another high-profile murder case without a body resulted in the 1996 conviction of Thomas Capano, a rich, well-known Delaware lawyer who was charged with killing his mistress, Anne Marie Fahey, the appointments secretary for Governor Thomas R. Carper. Her political connections likely ensured that her case, despite lacking a body, wouldn't be brushed under the rug.

Capano's own brother, Gerard Capano, testified on behalf of the prosecution that he and Capano took a boat off the coast of New Jersey and dumped a woman's body into the water. Thomas Capano was condemned to death, but seven years later the Delaware Supreme Court sent the case back for resentencing. The prosecution did not go after the death penalty the second time, and Capano is serving a life sentence.

But that was Delaware. In Illinois, said Peterson's attorney, Joel Brodsky, the laws make it very tough to prove a murder when no one can say for certain the victim is actually dead. Brodsky said his research shows prosecutors last succeeded in such a venture more than a hundred and fifty years ago, although this research seems to have missed the slaying of Stephanie Lyng and the murder conviction of her husband, Edward Lyng, seventeen years later. Nonetheless, Brodsky did not plan to represent the first man in a century and a half—that he knew of—to go down that way.

As it stood in the spring of 2008, Bretz did not believe the law would get as far with Peterson as he did with Bernal, for either the disappearance of Stacy or the death of Savio. That someone supposedly killed Savio seemed to be a compelling reason for prosecutors to charge Peterson with her murder. But, Bretz pointed out, switching hats to defense attorney, the finding alone is no proof that Peterson did it. If he were representing Peterson in such a trial, Bretz said he would call everyone from the initial investigation of Savio's death to testify about how they somehow missed the signs pointing to a homicide.

"You would certainly want to bring everyone who was involved in the accidental death [determination] and parade them in front of the jury," he said. "You would try to pull everyone you could involved in the first autopsy in front of the jury."

And then he would do his best to poke holes in the credibility of the autopsy performed on Savio's body after it spent three and a half years rotting in a grave.

"You would certainly want to use that to your advantage, and you'd want to hire your own expert to contradict the findings of the state's experts," he said.

"Any competent defense attorney would be able to get an acquittal. Particularly as to the fourth wife, and even to the third. You really just have speculation. Even with them saying it's a homicide, you don't have any evidence tying him to it."

Switching back to the prosecution's table, Bretz said he "would be analyzing very carefully all the statements [Peterson] has made, particularly the time frame of when Stacy disappeared. At some point in this type of investigation, what they're hoping for is some kind of breakup, some kind of slipup."

Even better, he said, would be some clue surfacing "that ties him to the scene" or "a witness stepping forward or a piece of forensic evidence."

But based on what he's seen so far, Bretz said, there's not a whole lot to stock a prosecutor's arsenal.

"Without knowing exactly what they have, at this point, it's potentially a case we may never see indicted, unless some more comes into the picture," he said.

With a high-profile case such as this one, which the national media pounced on within days of Stacy's disappearance and months later showed no sign of releasing, public opinion and political consequences doubtlessly come into play.

"I'm not saying the prosecutor's office is controlled by the press," Bretz said. "But they're certainly mindful of the press."

Additionally, Glasgow was up for reelection in 2008, only adding to the pressure for him to pull the trigger on Peterson. But Bretz did not believe Glasgow would shoot recklessly.

"I don't think a seasoned state's attorney who has been around for some time now would do that," he said. "He's done fairly well in the polls without doing something like that. We don't charge people unless we can prove them guilty beyond a reasonable doubt."

After all, Glasgow, like any prosecutor, has but one opportunity to go after a target, so he'll only want to head into the courtroom with a strong case.

"If you charge [someone] and go to trial and lose, then you have a double-jeopardy situation," Bretz said, referring to the practice, prohibited by the Fifth Amendment to the U.S. Constitution, of trying someone twice for the same crime. "You only get one shot at it." In Bretz's opinion, voiced in late March 2008, the time had not yet come to take that shot. Glasgow, he said, had no case against Peterson.

"If they don't have substantially more than what we've heard about in the media," he said, "it would not surprise me if Peterson is not charged in either one of these cases."

Even if police and prosecutors do not come up with substantially more than what has been heard about in the media, they might be able to dive through a loophole—so long as the Illinois House of Representatives is able to open one up for them.

In April of 2008, State Senator A.J. Wilhelmi of Joliet—with the support of Glasgow—sponsored a bill which would allow prosecutors to enter into evidence relevant statements from witnesses who were killed, threatened, or bribed to prevent them from testifying.

"We should be able to use the tools already available at the federal level and in nearly a dozen other states to fully prosecute criminals," said Senator Wilhelmi. "This bill gives prosecutors the ability to use evidence that a criminal defendant actively tried to eliminate. The goal of this legislation is to make sure that the full truth is heard by the jury."

While neither Glasgow nor Wilhelmi has publicly said the legislation was cooked up specifically with Peterson in mind, some close to the case have come to call it "Drew's Law." And there were others who questioned its constitutionality.

Senate Bill 2718 had yet to become a state law by the summer of 2008, however, and Peterson was still a free man.

Looking at the case as neither a prosecutor nor as a defense attorney, but simply as someone stuck doing his or her civic duty, Bretz still does not think the evidence against Peterson holds water.

"If I was sitting on the jury myself and the evidence was as it is, I would have to find [him] not guilty," he said.

Any prosecutor hates losing a high-profile case, but Glasgow could feasibly go after Peterson and, if things fell apart, blame failure on his political nemesis.

Glasgow was not in office when Savio was found dead in her dry bathtub in March 2004. The state's attorney at that time was his Republican rival, Jeff Tomczak, who soundly defeated Glasgow in the November 2000 election.

The vicious campaign left bad feelings on both sides, but four years later Glasgow rose from the ashes and took down Tomczak to win back his job. Tomczak's campaign was hobbled when his father, former Chicago Water Department boss Donald Tomczak, was hit with federal charges alleging he had collected thousands in bribes from trucking firms. Donald Tomczak's arrest came less than two weeks before his son faced off with Glasgow on Election Day.

The arrest of Tomczak's father was not the only startling development to occur shortly before that election. Within a week of voters casting their ballots, detectives with the Will County Sheriff's Department arrested Kevin Fox and charged him with the heinous sexual assault and murder of his three-year-old daughter, Riley. The day after the arrest, Tomczak said he was pursuing the death penalty for Fox. The unusual alacrity with which he came to that decision was widely denounced, and he was criticized for allegedly rushing the case to garner good publicity prior to the election.

If this was the case, it did not help. He still lost to Glasgow. Then, in June of 2005, Glasgow freed Fox after DNA testing performed by a private laboratory excluded Fox as the source of saliva found in Riley's body. Fox and his wife went on to score a fifteen-and-a-half-million-dollar award in a civil case against the detectives and the county.

Glasgow turned loose a man who a jury concluded should not have been arrested, who had been jailed under his rival's regime, and the enormous settlement in the Fox civil suit must serve as a caution against proceeding hastily in a case. Certainly there's also the fresh memory of Mike Nifong, who prosecuted three Duke University lacrosse players on charges of rape, kidnapping, and sexual offense, only to have the case blow up in court due to a lack of evidence and an accuser who changed her story. The three players were declared innocent, and Nifong was fired and disbarred.

In the Fox affair, Glasgow came out on top of Tomczak, but more than three-quarters of the way through the second coming of his administration, he has prosecuted no one for the little girl's death. Likewise, by the spring of 2008, months away from another election challenge, Glasgow also was charging no one for the death of Savio or the disappearance of Stacy. Armed with Blum's opinion that someone killed Savio, as well as with the testimony of her relatives, who insist she feared Peterson and predicted he would do her in, Glasgow could certainly jail Peterson, possibly right before election time, and charge him with his third wife's murder.

If things go well for Glasgow in the courtroom and his office ultimately wins a conviction, he can say he is the man who stepped up and put away a killer, who did the job Tomczak should have done in 2004. And if Tomczak had done his job when he should have, Glasgow could crow, maybe Stacy Peterson never would have disappeared.

In the event that Peterson is acquitted and walks free, Glasgow could blame Tomczak for the outcome. It would be easy to make excuses, to say the case was too hard to prove, considering the length of time between Savio's death and the case being taken seriously by the state's attorney's office. As far as Stacy's case, Glasgow could always point out that without a body it may not be prudent to proceed. As Bretz said, the prosecution gets but one crack at putting a killer away.

Bretz contends that Glasgow is above charging Peterson solely for the political punch it would pack in an election year. In any event, Glasgow does not appear to be in a tough reelection battle. His opponent, former Assistant State's Attorney Judy DeVriendt, has run a strangely quiet campaign. In fact, for a political candidate, she's been practically invisible.

Maybe DeVriendt wanted it that way. There were some who said she played a part in Glasgow's loss in 2000. DeVriendt was working for Glasgow when the state's attorney's office had sheriff's deputies remove a baby boy from the custody of his mother and hand him over to a man claiming to be his father. The case drew harsh criticism and led to DeVriendt's suspension and termination. She fought to get her job back and was reinstated, but then resigned. The baby was reunited with his mother after a few days, but Tomczak used the case to hammer away at Glasgow in the 2000 election. After losing, Glasgow conceded that the baby case contributed to his downfall, even if the public perception—that he wrested a baby from the arms of his mother—was not the reality.

But with DeVriendt's lack of visibility and most famous case an embarrassment that led to her getting fired, Glasgow does not appear to have significant reason to worry about his reelection chances. Not enough, at least, to do anything as rash as arresting Drew Peterson before he feels he has a strong enough case.

DeVriendt, it should be noted, was not the only one who left Glasgow's office under a cloud. Bretz did himself, after getting tangled up in a scandal with former Judge Patricia Schneider, with whom he had worked in private practice, and her brother, developer Edward Mattox, whom Bretz represented.

Soon after he started as the first assistant state's attorney in December 1992, Bretz authorized a felony sex abuse charge against a twenty-year-old man, who had gotten Mattox's teenage daughter pregnant. While a felony charge required the man to be at least five years older than the girl, and he was only a little more than four, he was still arrested and jailed.

As a result, Bretz was convicted of the misdemeanor charge of "attempted official misconduct." He was convicted of a second count of the same charge in connection with assisting a friend of Schneider and Mattox during an investigation of illegally stored hazardous waste at an auto repair shop. In this unrelated incident, Bretz kept the case file in his office, resulting in the probe being suspended.

Schneider was convicted of felony official misconduct and was disbarred. Bretz took a three-year suspension. He returned and rose to prominence in the local legal community.

As a defense attorney, Bretz was puzzled by the way Peterson's lawyer handled matters.

"The one thing that has been somewhat surprising to me is that his attorney has not told him to keep a lower profile," Bretz said.

"I don't know if they're just trying to counteract the negative press and trying to personalize him." If so,

Bretz doesn't think it's working, because he sees Peterson coming off as "arrogant and shallow."

"I would have insisted he put a stop to that long ago," he said. "And I'm not the only one who thinks that. I've talked to other seasoned criminal defense attorneys out of Chicago. They're saying, 'What's up with his attorney?' I don't know. They wonder if he's into it for the publicity. I don't know what their fee arrangement is."

Regardless of how much or how little Peterson is paying for Brodsky's services, Bretz did not seem to think Peterson was getting his money's worth. Peterson would be much better served by a lawyer who instructed him to mouth such non quotes as "No comment" or "We'll win the day in the end."

"Whether he had nothing to do with the death of his third wife and the disappearance of his fourth, people would expect you to be more somber about it, and he has clowned around," Bretz said, pointing out the ardor with which Peterson spoke about the radio-show dating game.

"A lot of people found that distasteful," Bretz said. "I could see the police and the prosecutors almost coming unglued about that thing.

"If anything, I think that the police and the prosecutors will almost be more driven by the arrogance of the whole thing. If you perceive, as a police officer or a prosecutor, that someone is talking to you or acting like he's above the law, it only makes you dig deeper to be more aggressive and look under every rock."

Bretz doesn't need to channel his past as an assistant state's attorney to imagine how he would react to Peterson's antics. They get under his skin now.

"As a human being, when you see a person clowning around, when the best case scenario to him, his wife has taken off and abandoned her kids, it's not really a laughing matter," he said. "I'm sure that if I was handling the case, that would be sticking in my craw, so to speak."

If he were in Brodsky's shoes, Bretz would attempt to portray Peterson in a positive light, as "a good father or something to that effect," but the key to his strategy would be keeping Peterson quiet and doing the talking for him.

"The traditional school of thought in criminal defense is, you don't want your client to make any statements to anyone about anything," Bretz said. And you particularly don't talk to the police.

"I usually tell my clients, whether they offer you the winning lottery ticket or stick a gun to your head, I tell them not to say anything without their attorney present."

The press follows the police on Bretz's list of people not to talk to.

"One of the dangers is people write down what you say, but it's slanted to their point of view," Bretz said.

Any speaking to the media should be done, or at the very least directed, by the attorney. Bretz explained how he would handle Peterson.

"Come across as being concerned," he said. "The loving husband.... 'Stacy, please come back to me. I know we've had our differences, but please come back to me. I love you. The children....' We haven't heard any of that.

"I would have just taken a completely different approach to it," he said, adding, "preferably, I would have done all the talking."

Bretz said he has encountered difficult clients before, and even let the ones who dismissed his instructions go, but "for the most part, people listen to you."

The point Bretz tries to get across to his clients is the police only care about what you say if they can use it against you. They are looking for incriminating statements or a statement they can prove untrue, he said. It's not as if you are going to talk your way out of trouble in the papers or on television.

"If the police have enough in fact to arrest you, they're going to arrest you whether you say anything or not," he said.

If he were representing Peterson, Bretz said he would try to establish that Stacy was still alive or had made plans to take off alone. Failing that, he said, "Your best bet is to sit back, say little, stay out of the limelight, let the investigation take its course, and hope it hits a dead end."

Immediately after Stacy was reported missing, her family expressed a distrust of the police, which seemed understandable considering that Peterson himself was a cop, and he'd apparently skated without serious scrutiny when his last wife died.

"The only thing we worry about is, once a cop, always a cop," Matthew Simmons, the husband of Kerry Simmons, who is a half sister of Tina Ryan, said to me on November 1, 2007, while we stood in the midst of the mayhem outside Peterson's residence. The day we spoke, police pored over the house searching for clues to Stacy's disappearance.

Simmons had some advice for the police as they combed for clues, going so far as to let the air out of the inflatable Halloween decorations in the front yard and to check beneath the family's aboveground swimming pool.

"It's just like this," he said. "Do your job. That's all we're asking."

That same day, Savio's sister Anna Marie Doman showed up and decried what she described as the indifference of the state police who had investigated her sister's death in 2004.

"Nobody looked at my sister's case close enough," Doman told me. "I never got a call back [from the police]. It was like they couldn't be bothered."

About a week later Doman learned that the investigation into her sister's death was being reopened. The day before Savio's body was exhumed, Doman's son, Charlie Doman, said he didn't want the Illinois State Police to investigate his aunt's death again, because he remembered how they had handled it the first time.

"I think another agency needs to look at it," he said. In explaining why, he said, "Well, they fucked up. Now what are they going to do about it?" He also wondered, "If they're protecting this guy, why are they protecting this guy? Does he have something on them?"

Doman didn't get his wish; the investigations into Savio's death and Stacy's disappearance remain in the hands of the state police. Whatever they were doing about either case, they've said little about it publicly. On the one occasion they let the press in on what they trumpeted as a possible break, it blew up in their collective face, with the hot lead proving to be nothing more than a truck driver's fabrication.

Peterson's former boss, Bolingbrook Police Chief Ray McGury, was more candid about the case. He publicly shared his desire to fire Peterson—a possibility his sergeant dodged by retiring—and his disgust at his subordinate's antics after his wife disappeared. Unlike Bretz, McGury was confident Drew Peterson would be charged in connection with both Savio's death and Stacy's disappearance.

"They're just waiting for some things to happen," McGury said in January 2008. "Some things have to happen. Some information has to come back to them to start putting some pieces in place."

McGury believed there would be a resolution to both cases. He also was of the mind that Stacy knew what part her husband might have played in the death of his third wife. In fact, he believes she might have known all along.

"I think she did," he said. "And that's that tightrope you walk, because she's a victim and yet, you know...."

Stacy was Peterson's alibi when the state police investigated Savio's death, an official told me. Once she was nowhere to be found, his alibi was gone. Then again, as long as she didn't turn up, she couldn't recant her story either. If McGury's theory ends up playing out, Stacy and Savio are both victims, but Stacy had a hand in at least covering up for her husband. She might not have known what she was getting into when she wed Peterson, but if McGury was right, she learned before too long.

"The day, and this is my personal opinion, the day she married him was the day she signed her death warrant," McGury said. "Personal opinion: She's a young girl at the time. What was she, eighteen when she married him? I've got a son that's twenty. He's a kid.

"But still, I can kind of see. I do want to give her the benefit of the doubt. I think she got caught up. She came from a tough life, at least I understand that she did. She had a guy who was good to her, who had money—took care of her. [It] was the first time probably in her life that she had that. There are thousands of stories like that I'm sure in this country, where people get sucked up into that whole scenario there."

Stacy might have been one in a thousand, but the other nine hundred ninety-nine were not the focus of months of national media scrutiny. For a time, her story dominated not only all local outlets, but was also daily fodder for cable-news programs that breathlessly reported every new development or rumor in the case, however minor or unlikely. Sharon Bychowski practically devoted her life to keeping the public aware of the missing woman's case, but all that attention amounted to little in regard to helping unravel the mystery of where her best friend Stacy had gone.

While rumors swirled that the police and prosecutors were ready to pounce on Peterson and charge him with the murder of his fourth wife—just as soon as they could find her body—they had a body all along in 2004. But the state police insisted that this body, of third wife Kathleen, ended up dead accidentally.

Television talking heads were quick to cast aspersions on Will County Coroner Patrick O'Neil for supposedly botching the inquest into Savio's death. But O'Neil merely presided over the proceeding. During the inquest, Savio's relatives painted a frightening and sinister picture of Peterson, but Illinois State Police Special Agent Herbert Hardy informed the six-member coroner's jury that nothing indicated that Savio had met her end through foul play. Savio drowned after falling and hitting her head in the tub. It was as simple as that. The jury heard this and returned with a determination that Savio was indeed the victim of an accidental drowning. It is hard to question their conclusion in light of Hardy's testimony.

The results of a coroner's inquest carry absolutely no weight in criminal court. Yet, for some reason, the state police chose to point to it as the reason to close the case on Savio's death.

For the state's attorney to ever charge Peterson, the state police will have to explain what their agents were thinking in 2004. Such a move by prosecutors would be tantamount to throwing the investigators under the proverbial bus, since in criminal trials prosecutors and police play for the same side. Even if the agents on the case deserve to be thrown there, it's a step any politician would have to be reluctant to take.

Drew Peterson must be nervous. He likens his position to being stricken with cancer and waking up each day hoping a miracle cure has been discovered. But it is not clear if he means that this miracle cure will be Stacy coming home to show everyone he did not kill her; that the state police will bungle the investigation of her disappearance—just as they did with his last wife, if forensic pathologists Michael Baden and Larry Blum are to be believed; or that he is brought to trial and found innocent.

Whatever Peterson believes about the mess he has gotten himself into—or the tough hand fate has dealt him to play—he remains free to talk about it with whichever reporter happens to show up at his front door, or on whatever television program he deigns to grace with his appearance. For no other reason than that many people think he killed two women he had married, Drew Peterson is a man in demand.

In March of 2008, he also bested the state police in court to get back his seized Grand Prix, Denali and computers. Drew was being Drew, the cop who in the 1980s was fired and indicted, only to have the charges dropped and his job restored. Twenty years later he was under suspicion for his third wife's death; nothing came of it. Then his fourth wife vanished, and so far no one can stick anything criminal about that on him. The state police take away his computers, guns and cars, and he gets back everything but the guns. And even the guns, or at least most of them, ended up in the possession of his son Stephen, as Peterson requested. He is Drew Peterson, and he keeps winning.

And this is where the expert lawyers have nothing to say to him, where maybe they are wrong and Brodsky is the best man to handle his case. Because no matter what the smart thing to do might be when you are suspected of killing a couple of your wives, Drew Peterson, the man in demand, has seldom failed to meet these demands. Whether he does it himself, showing up in New York to make a live morning show appearance or tape a prime-time spot, or sends Brodsky, Drew Peterson and his lawyer have said too much and too many of the wrong things. Yet Peterson is still walking around saying them.

Peterson may actually feel like he has cancer, but in the end he is probably going to be all right. Considering Peterson's history of slipping out of trouble, Glasgow's lack of a strong opponent in the upcoming election to spur him toward taking action, and the stubborn elusiveness of a body that can be identified as Stacy, the incumbent state's attorney may be content to watch public interest wither and die, and embark on another four years in office.

Drew Peterson was a cop. He knows how the system works. He has testified in court more times than he can remember. He has told me that appearing before a grand jury is old hat to him. Peterson knows how the deck is stacked. And no matter what he says about his anxieties and worries, he can't be that scared.

EPILOGUE

In the months since her best friend vanished, Sharon Bychowski has done her very best to antagonize Drew Peterson.

She's rallied the community, organizing benefits and fundraisers to subsidize volunteer searches for Stacy Peterson. She's plastered the windows of her house, right next door to Drew's, with missing-person fliers and erected a large sign in her front yard bearing Stacy's photograph under the words "Where is Stacy???" In an expression of neighborhood solidarity, the sign moved around to other houses on the cul-de-sac of Pheasant Chase Court. And Bychowski rarely misses an opportunity to speak against Peterson in the media, slamming him for everything from hiring a publicist to supposedly socializing with young women apparently star-struck by his notoriety.

"He's a married man," she said. "We need to remind him of that."

In his newfound bachelorhood, Peterson has stepped out every once in a while on weekends—sometimes in the company of his attorney, Joel Brodsky, and his friend from up the street, Steve Carcerano—and passed some time at Tailgaters, a neighborhood bar. Bychowski took issue with his leaving his four kids home alone, even though his sons born to Kathleen Savio were by then teenagers and old enough to watch the younger two.

To remind Peterson of his status as legal husband of Stacy, Bychowski and her son, Roy Taylor, organized a "boycott" of Peterson's hangout, calling for patrons to walk out if he dared to set foot inside. Instead of going back, Peterson, Brodsky and Carcerano took their business to Chicago's upscale Gibsons Bar & Steakhouse. At Gibsons, Brodsky said, Peterson would be "able to meet a much nicer class of people."

Peterson still managed to find himself in the company of a very attractive, and very young, woman. Kim Matuska, an employee of the tanning salon frequented by Peterson's friend Steve Carcerano and then Peterson himself, told me she had on occasion spent the night at Peterson's home—although she insisted there was "nothing physical" going on. When I asked him about it, Peterson did not seem to share that opinion.

Either way, Peterson was there for Kim when the Naperville police pulled over the guy she was riding with one early May morning and took him into custody. She and Peterson happened to be talking on the phone at the time. They were talking on the phone a lot around then, she said, and he rushed out about 2 o'clock in the morning to pick her up. He rushed out so fast, in fact, that the Naperville police stopped him for speeding. Peterson got off with a warning.

Matuska, an aspiring veterinarian attending a community college in the Chicago suburb of Glen Ellyn, said the cops had hassled her about her involvement with Peterson—right after her very own mother called them about it.

Matuska said a state police investigator showed up at the tanning salon and told her that not only was he sure Peterson killed both Kathleen and Stacy but that she would be next. Amazingly, the young woman was not put off by this and asked the cop what was actually a very valid question: "Then why isn't he in jail?"

Nearly a month into Matuska's relationship with Peterson, even Sharon Bychowski—Peterson's most determined opponent—had yet to talk any sense into her.

But after months of squaring off with Peterson, Bychowski became terrified of her neighbor, and for good reason: The suspect in two homicides had acquired the ability to open her garage door.

A remote control garage door opener programmed for Bychowski's residence was inside one of Peterson's vehicles that the Illinois State Police had seized as evidence in November 2007. In March 2008, Peterson managed to recover the Pontiac Grand Prix and GMC Denali, and when going through the cars, he discovered the opener that Sharon had given to Stacy so that she could get inside to prepare for a garage sale. Now Peterson had the opener, and he used it to open her garage door.

"I fear for my life," Sharon told me after seeing, to her alarm, her garage door mysteriously open and figuring out why.

"In the event that anything happens to me, I want the public to know I fear for my life. I feel closer to Stacy and Kathleen than ever."

Bychowski called the police, who tried to get Drew to give up the garage door opener. He refused. It was his property, he said. Besides, he was only checking the openers when he was looking through the cars that he had just gotten back from the police. He had no idea it would open Bychowski's garage.

"It's nothing I did intentionally," he said. "So kiss my ass."

That would not be Peterson's only brush with the law after Stacy went missing. In fact, he would end up under arrest on a felony charge of unlawful use of a weapon when police and prosecutors decided—nearly seven months later—that one of the guns taken into custody as possible evidence in Stacy's disappearance was illegal.

The barrel of the weapon, which was a semi-automatic assault rifle Brodsky claimed Peterson carried with the department's blessing as part of his SWAT duties, was shorter than the state-mandated sixteen inches. Peterson surrendered himself at the Bolingbrook police station and was driven to the Will County jail in Joliet by a couple of state troopers. He seemed to be enjoying himself on the ride, laughing heartily and scoffing at his latest legal jam as nothing more than "the usual."

Peterson spent only a few hours being processed in the county jail and was released after posting a $7,500 bond. On his way out, Peterson exclaimed, "There's good news—I just saved a bundle on my car insurance!"

One cop source questioned why the prosecutor charged the case at all and mocked Will County State's Attorney James Glasgow for waiting so long to do so. The source wondered how prosecutors could have suddenly realized the gun was illegal after holding onto it for more than a year.

"What?" the source asked. "Nobody had a ruler seven months ago?"

A spokesman for Glasgow said prosecutors were well aware all along that the gun was illegal and only took action when it appeared they might lose custody of it and some of the other weapons they were holding in the case. It turns out prosecutors might have been right about that, as the very next day, Brodsky won the return of eight guns being held by police for evidentiary purpose. Possession of the weapons was transferred to Peterson's son Stephen, the Oak Brook cop.

While Peterson laughed his way in and out of police custody, for Bychowski her neighbor's return was no laughing matter. With one push of a garage door opener, he frightened her enough to install video cameras on the exterior of her house and inside her garage.

The posters and signs in Bychowski's yard, however, seemed to truly get under Peterson's skin. He said he worried about the effect the pictures would have on his two youngest children, Anthony and Lacy. They would ask him, "Why is that picture there?" Peterson said. The whole time Stacy has been missing, he's continued to tell them their mother is on vacation.

"I tell them the picture's up because they miss her," Peterson said. "I don't tell them they put them up to harass me. My whole thing is, do what you want to me, but leave the kids alone."

While Peterson was feuding with one next-door neighbor, the other was hoping to pull stakes and get out of the cul-de-sac. In the wake of Stacy's disappearance, those neighbors put their three-bedroom, two-and-a-half-bath house up for sale. As of March 2008, the house was still on the market.

The life of Drew Peterson has certainly taken a drastic turn since October 28, 2007, ten days after the fourth anniversary of his fourth marriage. A week and a half after he'd sprung for a diamond ring as an anniversary gift for his wife, he was insisting to a skeptical world that he had nothing to do with her puzzling and troublingly abrupt disappearance. By the time the long Illinois winter, one of the snowiest in years, was slowly giving way to spring, Peterson had been in the national news so much that he was beginning to sound like Princess Diana or George Clooney, a major celebrity fed up with his fame, instead of a lifelong suburban cop who became a media spectacle because most of America believed that he might have killed his last two wives. He bemoaned his lack of privacy, how he could not even escape his notoriety in Disney World and the way his house was pelted with eggs while he was out of town.

Life on Pheasant Chase Court has also been transformed. A neighbor across the cul-de-sac from Peterson was more galled by the press than by having a suspected killer on the other side of the street. In the midst of the media siege of late 2007, the woman living there barked at reporters to get off her grass. Someone then strung yellow caution tape around her lawn. Long after the television crews, cameramen, reporters and satellite trucks had departed from Pheasant Chase Court, the caution tape remained, warning no one to stay away from the grass.

The caution tape, the missing-persons signs and fliers, Bychowski's video cameras, Peterson himself—all were still on Pheasant Chase Court while, down in Joliet, a grand jury continued to investigate the death of Kathleen Savio and the disappearance of Stacy Peterson. Until Drew

Peterson was either charged or exonerated, until there was some definitive response from the criminal justice system about his role in the fates of his last two wives, it seemed Pheasant Chase Court and probably all of Bolingbrook would be in limbo.

Peterson himself would likely welcome a resolution, although, of course, one in his favor. In the months since Stacy's disappearance, he's been the subject of stares and dirty looks, of whispers and accusatory murmurs. His friend Steve Carcerano once let me know that it was important for him to accompany Peterson to a bar or restaurant so that he could be "the eyes" in case "somebody tries to stick a knife in Drew's neck." Brodsky, too, told me he'd received numerous insulting messages, some of which ended along the lines of "I hope you die." None of that seemed to dissuade Brodsky from pushing his case into the public eye; nothing appeared to cause him to question why he had taken it on in the first place.

Peterson wasn't fazed either. He laughed off the threats as he seemed to laugh off everything, from his wife's supposed infidelity to the next-door neighbor afraid he would kill her.

While Peterson and Brodsky still appeared in the news occasionally, at least Pheasant Chase was quiet again. For a time, the Bolingbrook street was like a Midwestern Modesto, California, from five years before. A media horde that would have dwarfed the legion outside Peterson's home overran the town of Modesto for a possibly more famous Peterson—Scott, whose wife, Laci, also went missing.

Less than four months after she disappeared, Laci and her unborn baby washed up on the shore of San Francisco Bay. Her husband's arrest followed in short order. Within two years, Scott Peterson was found guilty and sentenced to die, and Modesto residents could then begin putting the tragic episode behind them.

Bolingbrook remains without such resolution. No one has been charged in connection with the disappearance of Stacy Peterson or the death of Kathleen Savio. The lack of closure and the unanswered questions are troubling to some, traumatic to others. One day, Drew Peterson—or someone else—will have to tell Lacy and Anthony that their mother is not on vacation and that, in all likelihood, she is not coming back.

He has already addressed this with the other two children in the house, Thomas, who was fourteen when his mother was last home, and Kristopher, who was thirteen. Peterson says he has spoken with the boys, one of whom is now nearly as old as his stepmother when she was seduced by his father, and that they "know" what happened with Stacy. He has let them in on the fact that she ran off with another man.

But someone will have to explain to the two boys why their stepmother, who legally adopted them after their real mother suddenly died, never came back for them; why she never bothered to write a postcard or make a telephone call. Someone will have to try to convince them that their new mother fled from her home to indulge herself in an adulterous romance instead of simply divorcing her husband, taking a good portion of his assets in the process, and undoubtedly keeping custody of half, if not all, of the four children. The boys might have questions about this someday.

And there might be answers to these questions, but they are likely about as plausible as a married mother of four embarking on a ten-month vacation, as her youngest children, sadly, supposedly believe. And as sad as it might be for a two- and three-year-old to grow up without their mom, they at least have lost only one mother. Thomas and Kristopher have lost two.

POSTSCRIPT

In July 2008, Paula Stark and Len Wawczak, married acquaintances of Drew Peterson, revealed to me that they had been recording their conversations with him for nearly seven months, at the behest of the Illinois State Police Department. They claimed that Peterson had made incriminating statements, which were recorded and would be vital to his arrest in connection with the death of Savio and the disappearance of Stacy—an arrest they were convinced would come after their undercover operation was exposed.

Peterson shut himself off from the media after Stark and Wawczak went public with their story, much like he did in the wake of Stacy's disappearance. He denied his former friends' insistence that he'd made damning statements in their presence, but his behavior suggested otherwise. Stark and Wawczak have stood by their story, although whether or not a conviction will result from their actions remains to be seen.

ACKNOWLEDGEMENTS

This book would not have been possible without the vision of my tireless agent, Jason Anthony, now of Lippincott Massie McQuilkin. Jason supported me every step of the way through the research and writing of this book. His unwavering encouragement, hard work and commitment got me to the finish line. I can't imagine a more dedicated agent. Thank you, Jason.

Special thanks to Michael Viner, Henrietta Tiefenthaler, Alina Poniewaz and everyone else at Phoenix for welcoming me to my new home. Your commitment to and belief in this book is deeply appreciated.

I am extremely fortunate to have had the assistance of Mary Jean Babic, formerly of Crest Hill. Mary Jean's experience as a journalist was invaluable to the writing of this book. Thank you so much for getting on the phone with me all of those midnights and helping me dot my "i's" and cross my "t's." Lou, you can have your wife back now.

And now that I got all of you out of the way, I want to thank my mother and father, Dorothy and Joe Hosey, for more than I could ever tell them. And to my sister, Sara Hosey, who has always been there: thanks.

To my girlfriend, Janet Lundquist, I cannot thank you enough for all of your hard work, patience, and kindness, not to mention the typing and tramping through Queen of Heaven cemetery in the rain. You helped me see the light at the end of the tunnel. To my daughter, Gracie Hosey, thanks for sitting in my lap and letting me write when I told you daddy had to work. This book is for you.

Alex Beck, you have been a good friend for a long time. Thanks for helping me out with this one, too.

Dan Haar, the metro editor of the *Chicago Sun-Times*, deserves thanks for keeping me on this story. Without Dan's commitment to covering the case, there would be no book. James Smith of the *Sun-Times* is a great designer and a better friend. Thanks for all of your help.

Dan Rozek, *Sun-Times* reporter, I am glad I got to meet you while covering this. Thanks for all the advice, conversation, and the cookies.

Sharon Bychowski helped me understand Stacy Peterson. Her concern for her and determination to not let her missing friend be forgotten is truly admirable. Thank you, Sharon, for helping me bring Stacy's story to readers. Candace Aikin and Roy Taylor also helped me fill in the blanks.

I am deeply indebted to the family of Kathleen Savio for their willingness to revisit painful memories in the interest of getting the story right. Anna Marie Doman, Charlie Doman and Melissa Doman: thank you all so much for your time and for your insights.

Bolingbrook Police Chief Ray McGury—thank you for your time and for your trust.

To the police and other officials who helped point me in the right direction and shared their knowledge, even when they were forbidden to, I can't thank you by name, but you know who you are. So thank you. The same goes for the ones from the other side of the law who took the time to explain their view of events. You know who you are as well. I am equally grateful.

Jody Hotchkiss of Hotchkiss & Associates found a Hollywood home for *Fatal Vows*. Thank you Helen Verno, Judith Verno and Winifred White Neisser at Columbia TriStar Television for your enthusiasm for the project.

I am grateful to Chuck Bretz for his legal insights into the case, and Dr. Philip Bonelli and Diane Wetendorf for their psychological ones.

Bob Darin and Bill Peters, I appreciate your help.

Finally, I must acknowledge Stacy Peterson and Kathleen Savio. Although you are not here to tell your stories, I hope I have done you justice.